THE GLUTEN-FREE QUINTESSENTIAL

Quinoa Cookbook

Eat Great, Lose Weight, Feel Healthy

THE GLUTEN-FREE QUINTESSENTIAL

Quinoa Cookbook

—— WENDY POLISI ——

SKYHORSE PUBLISHING

Skyhorse Publishing books may be purchased in bulk at special discounts for sales promotion, corporate gifts, fund-raising, or educational purposes. Special editions can also be created to specifications. For details, contact the Special Sales Department, Skyhorse Publishing, 307 West 36th Street, 11th Floor, New York, NY 10018 or info@skyhorsepublishing.com.

Skyhorse® and Skyhorse Publishing® are registered trademarks of Skyhorse Publishing, Inc.®, a Delaware corporation.

Visit our website at www.skyhorsepublishing.com

10 9 8 7 6 5 4 3 2 1

Library of Congress Cataloging-in-Publication Data available on file.

ISBN: 978-1-62087-699-2

Printed in China

Table of Contents

Appetizers & Snacks

Baking

Salads

Wraps, Burgers, Tacos & Sandwiches

Mains & Sides

Desserts

INTRODUCTION

Ten years ago, if you had told me that I would become a healthy, gluten-free cook, I would have told you that you had the wrong person. For starters, I didn't even know what gluten-free meant back then. With deep Southern roots and a love for all things gourmet, healthy and cooking weren't two words that I associated with each other. Ever. If it wasn't fit for the pages of *Southern Living* or *Bon Appétit* then it just wasn't for me.

I've never been good at sacrifices. I often joke to my readers that I just don't do deprivation . . . and I don't. Life's too short.

My road to healthy eating has been long and winding with lots of detours along the way. It probably would have never happened if I hadn't stumbled on the fact that real, healthy food actually tasted better than the processed packaged junk that I grew up on.

I became gluten-free because I feel better gluten-free. Like a lot of you, I don't have celiac or any real "disease" that demands I follow a gluten-free diet. My system just doesn't deal well with today's wheat and so I made the lifestyle choice to eliminate gluten from my diet. (More on that later.)

At the center of my gluten-free diet is quinoa. It's helped me lose weight and find health after thirty-five . . . and it can do the same thing for you!

Quinoa, Gluten & Your Health

Those of you who know me via my website (CookingQuinoa.net) know that, while I love quinoa, I'm not such an advocate that I believe it is the solution to all of your health problems.

I love quinoa, I think you should eat quinoa, but let's get real.

A healthy (gluten-free) diet demands variety and balance.

I encourage you to try quinoa and see if it can work for you in the same way it has worked for me, but I would never suggest that you need to eat quinoa every day to be healthy.

What I do encourage you to do is find healthy meals that you actually like and make them a regular part of your diet. Going gluten-free can be challenging and at times a bit discouraging. Rather than thinking about all the things you can't have, focus on adding the right foods to your diet.

Of course, I think quinoa is one of those foods. It is one of the healthiest foods that you can eat and, done right, it can also fill your need for comfort food.

I'm not a nutritionist and I'm not qualified to tell you what your diet should be. But I am someone who has lost a good deal of weight and someone for whom eating gluten-free has made a tremendous difference, so I will share with you what has worked for me.

Keep It Clean & Simple

Simplicity is critical on your journey to health, but simplicity and eating gluten-free don't always go hand in hand.

If you are transitioning to a gluten-free diet, now is a great time to focus on real whole foods that are naturally gluten-free. So many people use becoming gluten-free as an excuse to rely on packaged foods. I get the convenience factor, but for most of us the very reason that we follow a gluten-free diet is to improve our health. It just doesn't make sense to make processed gluten-free foods—many of which are packed with GMOs (genetically modified organisms)—the cornerstone of your diet.

Real foods will energize you and can also be quite simple. This is where quinoa really comes in hand! You can make a big batch over the weekend and it will last all week in the refrigerator. This means that you are never more than 15 minutes away from a simple salad or wrap.

If you are gluten intolerant and haven't been following a whole foods diet, you will be amazed at the difference eating right will make in your life.

My Story

I've made quinoa a key component in my real food diet and because of this it has made a significant difference in my road back to health. Although I'm nowhere near perfect, I can honestly say that I'm healthier in my forties than I was in my early thirties.

When I met my husband, I was twenty-six years old and there is no denying it: I was buff. I ran almost daily, lifted weights with the guys, and did kickboxing back when you had to go to a martial arts studio to find a class. I used to joke that if I didn't get bruises it wasn't a workout. Health was at the core of who I was—at least I thought so.

The problem is that I really didn't see the relationship between what I ate and my health. I thought that as long as I was working out five or six days a week, I was healthy.

I love food and we were lucky enough to be young and single, with both of us making good money. This coupled with our love for gourmet food and wine meant that one of our favorite things in the world to do was go out to nice dinners. And we did—often four or more nights a week. I never worried about calories and instead enjoyed the moment. In my mind I was young enough that it shouldn't matter.

When we weren't eating out, I was cooking gourmet meals at home. *Bon Appétit* was my best friend and back in those days the richer a dish was the better!

Flash forward six years.

I'm sitting in the doctor's office. It's a routine visit and I'm annoyed to be there. I'm thinking to myself "get the prescription for your birth control pills refilled and get out of here as soon as you can." (After all, we had dinner reservations that night!)

The nurse is taking my blood pressure and looks puzzled. She stops and looks at me in disbelief and doesn't say anything. She takes my blood pressure again. She leaves the room, still not saying anything. When she comes back she has another cuff and takes it for a third time. Finally she says, "Your blood pressure is really high."

Ok, I think. How high could it be? I'm thirty-two years old and while I wouldn't qualify as buff anymore, I'm still reasonably trim. I still get to the gym. Occasionally.

I then hear the number that will haunt me forever: 168/129.

I later find out that what this means as that the ripe old age of thirty-two, I was the proud owner of stage 3 hypertension.

This is long before I developed a mistrust of modern medicine, so I did what most people do. I blindly start popping pills twice a day. Pills that seem to drain my energy and make my brain fuzzy. I start to feel old.

Did I mention I was only thirty-two?

My weight started to creep up and despite this or the fact that I had such serious hypertension in the first place, not once did anyone mention my diet. No one suggested that I start exercising again. The only thing I ever heard was that I needed to take medicine. When pressed, my doctor told me that I should plan on needing medication to regulate my blood pressure for the rest of my life.

It wasn't until I got pregnant with my son and endured the joys of that high risk pregnancy that I even started to question this. I was on medication for my blood pressure for the entire pregnancy with my oldest. When he was five months old, I found out I was pregnant again.

Determined to NOT go through all the additional testing and screening I'd endured the first time, I did something that in hindsight was pretty stupid.

Luckily it worked out for me.

I started eating healthier and took myself off the medication. (Don't do this, by the way.)

I promised my OB that I'd take my blood pressure every day and if it was ever high I would go back on the drugs. Fortunately, it always hovered at just above normal— around 130/85—which wasn't considered to be high enough to warrant medication during pregnancy.

This pregnancy ended uneventfully and now I was the proud mommy of two boys, just fourteen months apart. I was in love with my babies, ecstatic, and exhausted—things that I'm sure all moms feel.

Two and a half years later everything in my life felt heavy.

The challenge of having two- and three-year-old boys was made even more stressful by the mortgage and real estate meltdown. The very industries that had paid for all those nice dinners out years before had all but vanished before our eyes and all that was left to do was pick up the pieces and try to move on.

At first, I ate my emotions and washed them down with wine after the boys were in bed. My weight ballooned up to 200 pounds. My high blood pressure returned, though I never went to the doctor for it. I was overwhelmed on every level and though I was only thirty-six years old, I honestly couldn't see the future.

It would be years before I would lose this feeling of being lost and sometimes it still haunts me. The truth is that poor health for many of us can be tied to how we feel about the rest of our lives.

You have to feel like you are worth the effort to eat healthy.

One of the things that helped me the most was finding Tosca Reno's Eat-Clean Diet series. At the time, I wasn't ready to really eat clean or even to figure out what worked for me. I still didn't feel that I was worth it. After all, I had two small boys who required my full attention and I allowed myself to believe that I was doing the best thing to put all of my energy into them. But it was the first time that it really sunk in that it was food that was at the core of my health. I made some small steps and it was here that I discovered quinoa.

It was love at first bite and over the next couple of years, the way I felt about food began to evolve. I started thinking about real food versus processed food. I stopped taking the boys to fast food restaurants and renewed my passion for cooking. Slowly, I was beginning to realize that I needed to question everything I'd been brought up to believe about food and find my own truths. I was still obsessed with gourmet food, but I was always thinking: how can I make this healthier?

My weight loss was very slow because I refused to follow any program that I couldn't follow for the rest of my life. I wasn't following a program, I was evolving as a person.

At first it was about a pound a month. Hardly impressive to those around you when you are starting off as heavy as I was! But I felt better and I was better for my boys. At thirty-nine I went vegetarian and it was with this move that I believe I said good-bye to high blood pressure forever. In the next year, without counting calories, consistent exercise, or ever depriving myself, I lost about two pounds a month. It was slow, it was steady, and it felt good!

I firmly believe that a plant-based diet can go a long way toward restoring health, but that isn't why I did it. I've never liked meat and for the first time I respected myself enough to start eating how I wanted rather than how I had been taught to eat. I think that when you start being true to yourself everything just starts to work. (I don't, by the way, feel that everyone should be a vegetarian. This is what works for me. Eating is a personal thing and I encourage you to figure out what works for you.)

As I write this, I am forty-one years old and expecting my first little girl to make her appearance in less than two months. My blood pressure these days hovers around 104/68 with no medication.

Not bad for a girl who was told nine years ago that she'd be on medicine for the rest of her life!

Don't underestimate the power of real food!

So Where Does Eating Gluten-free Fit In?

My road to becoming gluten-free was an unusual one. As I said earlier, I don't have celiac and I've never had a doctor tell me that I needed to be gluten-free.

CookingQuinoa.net was about two years old and I was constantly getting requests for gluten-free recipes. (This was after I'd written my first book, and to be honest I thought at the time that adding "OR gluten-free flour blend" to a gluten-free recipe was enough to make it work. It's not.)

I'd been having stomach problems for years, despite the fact that I ate fairly healthy. After hearing about the book *Wheat Belly: Lose the Wheat, Lose the Weight, and Find Your Path Back to Health,* by William Davis, I decided it was worth a read. I read it on a road trip from Arizona to visit family in Texas, and was struck by the fact that the modern wheat that we eat today barely resembles what my great-grandmother ate. This, thanks to major genetic modifications that happened in the 1960s and 1970s. According to author William Davis, M.D., "You cannot change the basic characteristics of a plant without changing its genetics, biochemistry and its effects on humans who consume it." Davis believes that today's wheat is causing all sorts of health problems in those that eat it—and not just those that suffer from the serious disease celiac. Some of these health problems include acid reflux, inflammatory bowel disease, skin disorders, asthma, and obesity.

Could this be the issue with my stomach? Or why my weight loss had finally stalled?

After talking it over with my husband, we agreed that the best thing for me to do was to remove wheat from my diet and see if I felt better.

It took me a couple of months to do this because for me, going gluten-free meant I also had to start blogging gluten-free. It kind of felt like a very public display of an entirely new way of eating—and one I wasn't all that confident in.

A few weeks in, I felt a little bit better, but I wasn't yet convinced that gluten-free was going to become a way of life for me.

It took a little more to convince me...

One day I was baking cookies for the boys. The recipe I was using was my own and it called for almond meal. I was short by ¼ cup and the easy solution was to substitute wheat flour. The kitchen was a mess at the time because I'd been cooking half the day and I ended up knocking the open bag of flour onto the counter, spilling it everywhere. Luckily it was right next to the sink, so I just used my hand to scoop the flour into the sink. About that time, I started sneezing so my flour-covered hand went up to my face in a natural reaction. I thought nothing of it.

About thirty minutes later, I was sitting outside with my husband and he asked me if I was feeling okay. At first I wasn't sure why he was asking, but then I noticed my face was hot and my hand was itchy. Both my face and the hand I used to clean up the flour were bright red, a little swollen, and itchy.

At first I was worried that my blood pressure was high again. It wasn't. Could it be a reaction to wheat?

I didn't want to believe it. Call it pride, call it fear of hypochondria, call it....whatever. I couldn't believe that I was one of those people who was impacted by wheat. It was fine that so many of my readers were gluten-free. I loved the challenge of gluten-free baking and I even planned on continuing to develop recipes that were gluten-free.

I just didn't want to have to BE gluten-free.

It took a little more convincing. There were several times after having been off gluten that I unknowingly had something with gluten in it and found myself sick. Although I knew that there was something to it for me, I still found myself wondering just how long I'd stick with it.

One day, after about two months off gluten I found my husband staring at me as if he was seeing me for the first time in a long while. I asked him what he was looking at and his reply shocked me. "I think there may be something to the whole gluten-free thing for you. You've lost more size around your middle than you did the entire time you were doing P90x."

This struck me for two reasons.

One, hubby isn't big on the fake compliments. I am someone who can go weeks without really looking at myself and his comment caused me to stop and look. Strangely, I could see what he was talking about. I weighed myself and discovered that I'd unknowingly dropped eight pounds—all of them seemingly from my middle.

And secondly, he is the world's biggest skeptic on diet trends. Though he saw merit in the whole wheat is not what it used to be argument, he was also very fearful that I was "creating" a condition for myself. If he was convinced there was something to it for me, I had to examine why it was that I was struggling so hard to accept that this was, like eating real food, what was best for me.

I wish I could say that this was the end of me "testing" gluten in my diet, but sadly I'm just too stubborn. At the end of the first trimester of this pregnancy I found myself too tired to cook. Slowly, gluten began to creep into my diet. My weight quickly shot up (prior to this point I hadn't gained any), my energy levels were at an all-time low and I was hopelessly miserable. Dense as I am, I failed to connect the dots.

Early in my third trimester my family members decided they wanted to go on a juice fast. Of course I couldn't participate, but I did want to do something to make an effort to be healthier. I decided that something would be getting back on the gluten-free bandwagon.

After about five days, it was as if a fog began to lift. Again, I didn't want to admit it but the truth was that my energy levels were up during a time in pregnancy when they should have been falling. For the first time in months, I was able to work again. My rapid weight gain stalled though baby has continued to grow. With my productivity soaring, I began to think and dream about the future—one I then knew would not include gluten.

Quinoa Nutrition

People who try quinoa for the first time often do so because they have been told that it is a nutritious (and gluten-free!) food that they should be including in their diets. Let's take a look at just what makes quinoa a "super food".

The Perfect Protein

Most people know that quinoa is rich in protein, but what is important to understand when you are talking about quinoa is that it isn't the quantity of protein that matters. (Although eight grams of protein per serving for a plant-based food is strong.) There are plenty of vegetarian foods that are rich in protein. Both wheat and oats have almost as much protein as quinoa.

Quinoa's nutritional significance is more about the quality of the protein than the quantity.

The reason that quinoa is so important is because it is a perfect protein—often called "complete." It contains all nine of the amino acids that we need for health. This is especially important to vegetarians and vegans, who in the past were encouraged to combine foods to meet their nutritional needs (a practice we now know is not necessary).

According to the Food and Agriculture Organization of the UN, the protein content of quinoa is equivalent in quality to that found in dehydrated whole milk. The UN states that quinoa is "the only plant food that contains all the essential amino acids, trace elements and vitamins and contains no gluten."

More than Just Protein

The health benefits of quinoa go way beyond just the exceptional protein content. It is rich in enzymes, phytonutrients, antioxidants, fiber, vitamins, and minerals. When you compare quinoa to corn, wheat, or barley, it is higher in calcium, manganese, phosphorous, zinc, potassium, copper, magnesium, and iron. Here are a few other things to know about quinoa nutrition.

- Phytonutrients and antioxidants are believed to help stabilize blood sugar levels.

- Quinoa is especially rich in manganese, which is known to activate enzymes for the metabolism of cholesterol and carbohydrates. It is also a great antioxidant that can help your body eliminate toxins.

- It is a good source of magnesium, which helps to relax blood vessels and muscles. This may be helpful for those with both migraines and high blood pressure.

- The fiber content of quinoa can help to tone your colon and is believed to work as a prebiotic, feeding microflora to your intestines.

- Most grain foods are very acidic, which is believed to cause health issues. (This is why we hear so much talk about following an Alkaline diet.) Quinoa is considered neutral, and is a good alternative for those who are concerned about a candida yeast overgrowth. Grains feed yeast and in some individuals can cause a systemic fungal infection with numerous health implications. This isn't an issue with quinoa.

A Look at Quinoa as Compared to Other Grains

Grain	Water	Protein	Fat	Carbohydrate	Fiber	Ash
Barley	11.1	8.2	1.0	78.8	.5	.9
Buckwheat	11.0	11.7	2.4	72.9	9.9	2.0
Corn	72.7	3.5	1.0	22.1	.7	.7
Millet	11.8	9.9	2.9	72.9	3.2	2.5
Oats	12.5	13.0	5.4	66.1	10.6	3.0
Quinoa	11.4	16.2	6.9	63.9	3.5	3.3
Rice	12.0	7.5	1.9	77.4	.9	1.2

Nutrient	Units	1.00 X 1 cup ------- 185g
Proximates		
Water	g	132.48
Energy	kcal	222
Energy	kJ	931
Protein	g	8.14
Total lipid (fat)	g	3.55
Ash	g	1.41
Carbohydrate, by difference	g	39.41
Fiber, total dietary	g	5.2
Starches	g	32.62
Minerals		
Calcium, Ca	mg	31
Iron, Fe	mg	2.76
Magnesium, Mg	mg	118
Phosphorus, P	mg	281
Potassium, K	mg	318
Sodium, Na	mg	13
Zinc, Zn	mg	2.02
Copper, Cu	mg	0.355
Manganese, Mn	mg	1.167
Selenium, Se	mcg	5.2
Vitamins		
Vitamin C, total ascorbic acid	mg	0.0
Thiamin	mg	0.198
Riboflavin	mg	0.204
Niacin	mg	0.762
Vitamin B-6	mg	0.228
Folate, total	mcg	78
Folic acid	mcg	0
Folate, food	mcg	78

Nutrient	Units	1.00 X 1 cup ------- 185g
Folate, DFE	mcg_DFE	78
Vitamin B-12	mcg	0.00
Vitamin A, RAE	mcg_RAE	0
Retinol	mcg	0
Vitamin A, IU	IU	9
Vitamin E (alpha-tocopherol)	mg	1.17
Tocopherol, beta	mg	0.06
Tocopherol, gamma	mg	2.20
Tocopherol, delta	mg	0.20
Lipids		
Cholesterol	mg	0
Amino acids		
Tryptophan	g	0.096
Threonine	g	0.242
Isoleucine	g	0.290
Leucine	g	0.483
Lysine	g	0.442
Methionine	g	0.178
Cystine	g	0.117
Phenylalanine	g	0.342
Tyrosine	g	0.154
Valine	g	0.342
Arginine	g	0.629
Histidine	g	0.235
Alanine	g	0.339
Aspartic acid	g	0.653
Glutamic acid	g	1.073
Glycine	g	0.400
Proline	g	0.444
Serine	g	0.326

Rye	11.0	9.4	1.0	77.9	.4	.7
Wheat	13.0	14.0	2.2	69.1	2.3	1.7

Source: Wood, R.T., "Tale of a Food Survivor: Quinoa," *East West Journal,* April 1985, pp. 64–68.

Here is a complete breakdown of the nutritional value of 1 cup of cooked quinoa:

Source: USDA National Nutrient Database for Standard Reference, Release 23 (2010), http://www.nal.usda.gov/fnic/foodcomp/cgi-bin/list_nut_edit.pl.

Get to Know Quinoa

Although the South Americans have been cooking quinoa for centuries, unless your parents were more than a little progressive in the culinary sense, chances are it isn't a food that you grew up eating. Since the 1980s, it has slowly but surely been gaining popularity in North America and other parts of the world.

At first it was simply a go-to protein source for vegans and die-hard health buffs. These days, however it is trending toward mainstream. It is not uncommon to find quinoa in the gluten-free or health food section of your grocery stores and you can even find it on the menu of healthier dining establishments.

Queen-what?

It's hard to get to enthusiastic about a food that you don't even know how to pronounce. Before we go on to talk about just what quinoa is, let's get that out of the way.

The correct way to say quinoa is "KEEN-wah."

What is quinoa?

Chenopodium quinoa is a member of the goosefoot family. Although you often hear it referred to as a grain, this is actually incorrect.

Quinoa is a seed that is related to plants like beet, chard, spinach, and the edible weed lamb's-quarter. Although the leaves can be eaten in the same way that you can eat spinach or chard leaves, it is the seeds that we commonly refer to as quinoa. If you were to classify quinoa, the correct classification is a pseudo-grain, that is, a non-grain that is treated like a grain in cooking.

One of the best things about quinoa is that it is non-GMO and has not been hybridized. In a world where GMOs should be a major concern for all of us, quinoa's purity makes it an attractive, staple part of our diets.

23

Can I grow quinoa?

Really, that depends on where you live.

Quinoa thrives in sandy alkaline soil that is generally considered poor for most crops. It loves high elevation and tolerates both freezing and the sun. The reason it is so frost resistant is the size of the germ, which is much larger than other grains (though remember, it isn't a grain).

Quinoa is native to Peru and Bolivia, but in the last twenty years, quinoa has been grown in many countries. It is now grown in Colorado and Canada, but a large portion of commercially available quinoa is still imported from South America. You see yellow quinoa most of the time, but red and black quinoa is also sold. There are actually some 1,800 varieties of quinoa!

History of Quinoa

Quinoa has an interesting and colorful history. It has been called many things including the "mother grain of the Andes," "Incan Gold," and "the mother of all grains." It is believed that quinoa has been cultivated since 3,000 BC in the high Andes Mountains.

In the time of the ancient Incas, quinoa was considered a sacred food. They referred to quinoa as *la chisaya mama* or "the mother grain." It was considered particularly important for pregnant and nursing mothers, as it was believed to improve milk supply.

Quinoa was the main component of the Andean diet, with animal protein falling into a secondary role. It is no surprise that a pound of seeds was enough to feed an Andean family of ten for a year on just one acre of land! Each growing season, the leaders would sow the first seeds with a golden trowel and prayers would be said for a good season. Armies would march for days with nothing more than "war balls" made up of quinoa and fat to sustain them.

The Fall of Quinoa

With the rise of the Spanish rule, the popularity of quinoa fell. The Spanish were not fond of quinoa and referred to it as "Indian food." They much preferred their own white rice. They also realized that quinoa gave the Incas strength, so they burned the quinoa fields and made it illegal to grow quinoa. As the act was punishable by death, the only place that quinoa survived was in the highest mountains of the Andes. Eventually, under the Spanish rule quinoa became nothing more than animal feed.

A Slow Rebirth

Flash forward to the 1970s and the history of quinoa is no less interesting. Quinoa was brought to the United State from South America by Don McKinley, who has been called the Quinoa Smuggler. He was working in South America as an importer and was immediately fascinated with quinoa. It was enough like rice that people would know how to prepare it, and it had sustained the Incas who ate very little meat for many years.

Although he saw its potential, it wasn't until the 1980s that he actively began working toward bringing quinoa to North America. Then living in Boulder, Colorado, he realized that there was a very good chance that quinoa would grow where he was. He sought out Steve Gorad, a colleague who traveled to Chile often and who was able to get him a 100-kilo sack of quinoa seeds.

Gorad move to Boulder and the two planted some of the quinoa seeds in their back yards. They then contacted Dwayne Johnson, a new crops agronomist at Colorado State University. He was impressed with quinoa as well—so impressed that he was later quoted as saying,

"If I had to choose one food to survive on, quinoa would be the best."

By 1982, McKinley and Gorad had nailed down the process of growing quinoa in North America. Quinoa Corporation was formed in 1983 as a joint venture with Sierra Blanca Associates (a non-profit agency). David Cusack became the corporation president, with Steven Gorad and Don McKinley on the board.

Between 1983 and 1987, just $76,000 of taxpayer money was spent developing quinoa as a new crop in North America. By 1995, the value of this crop was estimated at over $5 million and this has continued to increase. In addition to being successfully grown in the Colorado Rockies and Canada, quinoa is also being tested in the Pacific Northwest. According to the Food and Agriculture Organization of the UN, it is also "currently being cultivated in several countries in Europe and Asia with good yields."

Getting Started
How to Cook Quinoa

The first thing you need to know to get started with quinoa is how to cook it!

Within many of my recipes you will find instructions for cooking quinoa. In those cases, you will most likely see something like this:

1 cup quinoa, rinsed

This means that you are starting with dry, uncooked seeds.

Because quinoa absorbs flavors as it cooks so well, cooking it within the dish is a great way to kick the flavors up a notch.

There are times when this doesn't make sense, though. The perfect example is in a salad, where all the other ingredients will be raw. In these recipes, you will see something like this:

3 cups cooked quinoa

This means that you need 3 cups of quinoa that has already been cooked. To get this you will need to cook about 1 cup of quinoa.

Over time you may develop your own preferred way to cook quinoa, but in the meantime I suggest you give my method a try.

How to Cook Quinoa - The Basic Method

My method of cooking quinoa is a bit different from what you see on the package. I use lower heat and cook it a little longer which yields a fluffier quinoa that is perfect every time.

Step 1: Rinsing

The first thing that you want to do is rinse your quinoa. People ask me all the time if they can just skip this step. I get it. It is a bit of a hassle.

If you have purchased packaged quinoa, it may have been pre-rinsed. If it has been, it will clearly state this, very often in bold. (This is often a selling point.) If you buy in bulk or your package doesn't say that it is pre-rinsed you will need to rinse it. Even if the package says it has been rinsed, if you find yourself experiencing stomach distress after consuming it, chances are you need to rinse it.

Why Rinse?

The exterior of quinoa is covered in a substance called saponin. It is a natural pesticide that protects the plants as they grow. Unfortunately, as fantastic as it is in nature, it isn't so great on your plate. Saponin is extremely bitter and will also cause gastrointestinal distress for many people. It's pretty nasty stuff, so we want to get rid of it.

How to Rinse

Luckily, rinsing quinoa is very easy. The best tool I've found is a fine metal strainer. Place it over a bowl or the pot you plan to cook in. Add your quinoa and place it under a steady stream of water. (If you are worried about wasting water, you can always use the runoff to water your garden.) You will need to rinse the quinoa until the water runs clear.

If you don't have a strainer that is fine enough to rinse quinoa, you can use cheesecloth to line your strainer. I find this to be a bit cumbersome, but it does work.

Step 2: Cooking

> Now, you are ready to start cooking! You want to bring the quinoa and liquid to a simmer in a 1:1.25 ratio. To cook one cup of dry quinoa – which will yield 3 cups of cooked quinoa - you need:
>
> 1 ¼ cups cooking liquid (broth, water or juice)
>
> 1 cup quinoa, rinsed
>
> Bring the mixture to a simmer (the point just before a boil). Reduce your heat to low and cover. Cook the quinoa on the lowest setting your stove has for 35 to 40 minutes. Remove from the heat and allow to sit covered for 5 more minutes. Fluff and serve.

The 19-Minute Method

There are times when you may want to cook quinoa and you don't have 45 minutes to spare. As a busy mom of three, believe me when I say I understand this. Luckily, there is an easy solution that really doesn't sacrifice texture all that much. I've tried the traditional boil and simmer method, that you will find on the package as well as this method, and this is the one I prefer.

Step1: Rinse

Just like above, you will need to start by rinsing the quinoa. Sorry, no shortcuts there.

Step 2: Boil

Place your rinsed quinoa in a pot and cover it with water, juice or broth. Bring to a boil and boil uncovered for 9 minutes. Remove from heat and drain. Return to the warm pot and cover. Allow to sit covered off the heat for 10 minutes.

Baking with Quinoa Flour

Quinoa flour is absolutely amazing, though many people have been slow to realize just what a valuable addition it is to your kitchen. Its high protein content makes it especially valuable for gluten-free breads, as the protein helps with the structure and rise.

Why the widespread quinoa flour reluctance? Well quite simply, quinoa flour straight from the box has an odor that is off-putting to many people.

Yes, I know I've been criticized in the past for saying this (what with my being an advocate for quinoa and all!).

But if you are going to trust me to help you pick recipes for your family, I'm guessing you also expect a little honesty. So no sugarcoating here—I absolutely hate the way quinoa flour smells straight from the package.

For a long time I stayed away from it all together. Then I ran across the work of Linsey Herman, a food scientist who writes at CakeandCommerce.com. She discovered that by toasting quinoa flour you can eliminate the strong, grassy odor and bring out its rich nutty flavor.

How to Toast Quinoa Flour

1. Preheat your oven to 220 degrees.

2. Line 2 rimmed baking sheets with parchment paper.

3. Divide a 1-pound bag or box of quinoa flour among the baking sheets. You want to spread it out so that it is no more than ½ inch thick.

4. Place the baking sheets in the oven and cook for 2 ½ hours rotating the baking sheets half way through and stirring the flour to prevent burning.

5. Remove from oven and cool. Store in the refrigerator or freezer for best results.

Of course, you can skip toasting all together.

I just don't recommend you do so when you are trying to impress your mother-in-law with your culinary skills for the first time, in the event that she is one of those people who dislikes the smell of quinoa flour.

While we are talking about impressing people, I do have another word of caution for you:

Don't try substituting 100% of the flour in a given recipe with quinoa flour!

You will most likely be disappointed with the results. (The exception to this is in a non-baking dish where the flour is being used simply for binding.) Like other gluten-free flours, quinoa flour is best when mixed. Generally speaking, I use no more than 40% quinoa flour in a recipe, and I combine it with both starches and either xanthan gum or guar gum.

Baking Gluten-free

The science behind gluten-free baking is fascinating to me and I love playing with new flours. I'm guessing most of you aren't kitchen geeks like I am and would appreciate a little simplicity. To make things easier, I've come up with a gluten-free quinoa flour blend and I've tried to use it in as many of these recipes as possible.

Why so many flours?

Just about everyone who is new to gluten-free baking gets more than a little frustrated with just how many different flours it takes to get the job done.

I know. It's frustrating.

Unfortunately, trying to cut corners will just yield disappointing results. Although you can buy packaged flour blends, I encourage you to make your own. Not only is it much cheaper, but most prepared flour blends rely on brown rice flour as a staple ingredient. Although it may be fine in small quantities, because of the 2012 arsenic scare with rice, I prefer to stay away from it in most of my recipes. Here are the blends you will use with many of the recipes in this book:

Gluten-free Flour Blends

Gluten-free All Purpose Quinoa Flour Blend

1 ½ cups sorghum flour

1 ½ cups toasted quinoa flour

1 ½ cups corn or potato starch

1 ½ cups tapioca starch/flour

2 ¾ teaspoons xanthan gum

Mix all ingredients in a large container and store in the refrigerator.

Gluten-free Quinoa Cake Flour Blend

1 cup sorghum flour

1 cup toasted quinoa flour

¾ cup cornstarch

1 ½ teaspoons guar gum (or xanthan gum)

¾ teaspoon sea salt

Mix all ingredients in a large container and store in the refrigerator.

Making Quinoa Flour

Although quinoa flour is readily available at most larger grocery stores, natural food stores, and online, many people prefer to make their own quinoa flour.

Step 1: Rinse

The first thing you will want to do is rinse the quinoa. As tempting as it can be to skip this step, I don't advise it!

Step 2: Toast

Once your quinoa is rinsed, place it on a parchment-lined, rimmed baking sheet. Preheat your oven to 220 degrees and toast the quinoa for 2 ½ hours, stirring once to avoid burning.

Step 3: Grind and Sift

Once your quinoa has been toasted, place it in a grain mill, blender, or coffee grinder. (Note: Very small coffee grinders or inexpensive blenders may not grind it fine enough.) Process the quinoa until fine, and then place the flour in a fine metal strainer to sift out any seed fragments that remain. Store in an airtight container, preferably in the refrigerator or freezer.

Popping Quinoa

You may be surprised to know that you can pop quinoa in the same way that you can pop popcorn. Though it doesn't bulk up in the same way that popcorn does, it does expand slightly and experiences a fairly dramatic change in texture. Popped quinoa kind of reminds me of really small and slightly firmer Rice Krispies!

Dry Popping

This method allows you to pop quinoa without oil.

Heat a large skillet to high heat and add quinoa in a single layer, being careful not to crowd. As the kernels begin to pop, shake your pan. After 30 seconds to 1 minute, remove the pan from the heat. Allow it to sit in the pan for a minute more, watching to make sure it isn't burning. Transfer to another dish to prevent burning. Because all stoves heat a little differently, you may need to turn the heat down to avoid burning.

Popping in Oil

I love to use my electric (not air) popcorn popper to pop quinoa.

Plug your popcorn popper in and add a tablespoon of coconut oil. When the oil melts, add your quinoa and cover. Shaking every 10 seconds or so, pop the quinoa until it starts to turn golden brown. Unplug your popper and transfer to a separate dish to avoid burning.

Quinoa Flakes

Quinoa flakes are pressed quinoa seeds similar to what oatmeal is to oats. They are light in texture and good mixed into breakfast cereal, granola, and baked goods. You can purchase quinoa flakes in the gluten-free section of most larger grocery stores, at natural food stores, and online. If you can't find quinoa flakes, gluten-free oatmeal is a good substitution.

Your Healthy Gluten-Free Pantry

Flours

Brown Rice Flour

Rice flour is one of the most common gluten-free flours because at one time it was the only one readily available. It is fairly dense and can result in heavy baked goods. I tend to stay away from it because there is some controversy as to whether rice sold in the United States is healthy for consumption due to elevated arsenic levels.

Cornstarch

Cornstarch is an ingredient that I have a love-hate relationship with. On one hand, it offers very little in the form of nutrients. On the other, its importance to gluten-free baking is significant as it is key to providing a light texture.

Millet Flour

Millet flour is nutty and a little bit sweet. Like quinoa flour it is packed with protein and fiber.

Potato Starch

Not to be confused with potato flour, potato starch is a fine white powder that is a great alternative to cornstarch. It can be used in a 1:1 ratio to cornstarch and will yield a slightly heavier consistency. Potato starch is used as a part of a flour blend.

Quinoa Flour

Quinoa flour is milled from the seed. It is protein packed, offering a complete source of protein—something you don't see in most flours. The flavor of quinoa flour can be a bit strong, but toasting it helps it to mellow (see p. 28). As with all gluten-free flours, quinoa flour works best in a blend.

Sorghum Flour

Sorghum flour is a great addition to a gluten-free flour blend. It is high in protein and fiber and has a light, sweet taste.

Tapioca Starch

Tapioca starch helps to give baked goods a chewy texture. It works well with protein-dense flours like quinoa flour.

Xanthan (and Guar) Gum

Xanthan and guar gum are thickening agents that help gluten-free goods hold together. Without them your baked goods would be crumbly and not have the necessary structure to rise.

Considerations & Storage

If you have celiac or a serious gluten allergy, it is important that you source your flours from mills that use dedicated gluten-free facilities. Avoid buying from bulk bins as they may be contaminated.

All of the above flours are best when stored in air tight containers in the refrigerator or freezer. Allow to come to room temperature before using.

Substitutions

Egg Substitutions

If you are vegan or have an egg allergy, eggs can be substituted in all recipes. The result may be a bit denser, but using the following will help your baked goods hold together.

Flax Egg

Flax seeds are high in fiber and a great source of omega-3 fatty acids. Because whole flax seeds are not digestible, you should either purchase ground flax seeds or plan to grind whole flax seeds in your coffee grinder prior to using. To replace 1 egg, combine 1 tablespoon ground flax seeds with 3 tablespoons warm water. Stir well and set aside to thicken.

Chia Egg

Chia seeds are also a fantastic source of omega-3 fatty acids. To replace 1 egg, combine 1 tablespoon chia seeds with 3 tablespoons of warm water. Stir well and set aside to thicken.

Corn Substitutions

Baking Powder

If you have a corn allergy, it is important to make sure you use a corn-free baking powder. Most commercially available baking powders do not contain corn.

Xanthan gum

In place of xanthan gum, use guar gum.

Cornstarch

Use potato starch in a 1:1 ratio in place of cornstarch.

Breakfast

I used vegan Mexican chorizo, but any chorizo will do. Just make sure it doesn't have any hidden gluten!

Hash Brown Quinoa Casserole

Instructions:

1. Preheat oven to 450 degrees.

2. Spray an oven-safe, 10-inch skillet with canola oil and heat to medium high. Add chorizo and cook for 5 minutes, crumbling with the back of a spoon. Add garlic and cook for 1 minute longer. Remove from pan and combine with enchilada sauce.

3. Meanwhile, if using flax eggs combine 2 tablespoons of ground flax seeds with 6 tablespoons of warm water. Stir well and set aside.

4. Wipe pan clean and spray again with canola oil. (You want it to be well covered.) In a medium bowl combine cooked quinoa, shredded potatoes, onion, salt, pepper, and (flax) eggs. Add quinoa mixture into pan and press with the back of a large spoon or spatula. Cook over medium heat for 10 minutes—do not stir. Pour enchilada chorizo mixture on top of potatoes and top with shredded cheese.

5. Bake for 20 to 25 minutes, covering loosely with foil toward the end to ensure that the cheese doesn't burn. Allow to cool for 10 minutes and cut into wedges. Serve warm with desired toppings.

4 ounces gluten-free Mexican chorizo, casings removed
4 cloves garlic, minced
1 cup gluten-free enchilada sauce
2 cups cooked quinoa
3 pounds baking potatoes, peeled and shredded
½ cup finely grated onion
½ teaspoon sea salt
½ teaspoon fresh ground pepper
2 eggs beaten or flax eggs (2 tablespoons ground flax seeds + 6 tablespoons warm water)
4 ounces Daiya cheddar or cheddar cheese (1 cup)
For serving: salsa, guacamole, (vegan) sour cream, avocado slices, tomatoes

Servings 8, Calories 346, Fat 10.4g, Carbohydrates 51.6g, Protein 14.8g, Cholesterol 15 mg, Sodium 459mg, Fiber 7.6g, Sugars 3.5g

This is one of my favorite ways to start the day! I began using molasses upon the recommendation of my midwife, as it aids in iron absorption. Luckily, I found that I really like it. If you are someone who doesn't enjoy the taste, feel free to leave it off.

Apple Morning Start

Instructions:

In a medium saucepan combine oatmeal, quinoa, milk, molasses, salt, and ground cinnamon. Bring to a boil and then reduce to a simmer. Cook until the liquid is mostly absorbed and desired consistency is achieved, stirring in diced apple in the last 2 minutes of cooking. Remove from heat and stir in flax seeds. Transfer to serving bowl(s) and top with maple syrup and walnuts.

¼ cup oatmeal (regular or gluten-free)

½ cup cooked quinoa

1 cup almond milk or milk of choice

½ tablespoon organic blackstrap molasses (optional)

¼ teaspoon salt

½ teaspoon ground cinnamon

½ apple, diced or grated

1 tablespoon ground flax seeds or chia seeds (optional)

1 tablespoon maple syrup

1 tablespoon walnuts

Servings 2, Calories 211, Fat 6.7g, Carbohydrates 33.5g, Protein 5.7g, Cholesterol 0mg, Sodium 386mg, Fiber 5.4g, Sugars 13.6g

I love potatoes, and this recipe is one of my favorite ways to enjoy them at breakfast!

Quinoa Potato Pancakes

Instructions:

1. If using flax eggs, combine 3 tablespoons ground flax seeds with 9 tablespoons warm water. (Skip this step if you are using eggs.)

2. In a large bowl combine potatoes, carrot, quinoa, onion, and nutritional yeast.

3. Add (flax) eggs, flour, cayenne pepper, black pepper, and sea salt to potato mixture. Stir until well combined and form into small patties.

4. Heat oil over medium heat. Add patties and cook about 5 minutes per side, or until golden brown.

1 pound potatoes, washed and shredded
1 carrot, shredded
1 cup cooked quinoa
½ cup onion, chopped fine
3 tablespoons nutritional yeast (optional)
3 eggs or flax eggs (3 tablespoons ground flax seeds + 9 tablespoons warm water)
⅓ cup all purpose gluten-free flour blend (see p. 30)
¼ teaspoon cayenne pepper (optional)
½ teaspoon fresh ground black pepper
1 teaspoon sea salt
1 tablespoon coconut oil, for cooking

Servings 8, Calories 141, Fat 4.1g, Carbohydrates 20.5g, Protein 6.4g, Cholesterol 61mg, Sodium 269mg, Fiber 3.3g, Sugars 1.5g

Cherries are known to have anti-inflammatory compounds that can help with aches and pains and may also work to combat chronic disease. There is also research suggesting that tart cherry juice can help improve sleep.

Cherry Banana Quinoa Smoothie

Instructions:

In a blender combine quinoa flakes, cherry juice, almond milk, banana, flax, and vanilla extract. Process until smooth. Add in ice and process for another minute. Transfer to a glass and serve immediately.

¼ cup quinoa flakes

1 cup tart cherry juice

½ cup almond milk or milk of choice

1 banana, peeled and diced

1 tablespoon ground flax seeds (optional)

1 teaspoon vanilla extract

½ cup ice

Servings 1, Calories 389, Fat 5.8g, Carbohydrates 75.9g, Protein 7.1g, Cholesterol 0mg, Sodium 119mg, Fiber 8.6g, Sugars 44.5g

This healthy breakfast recipe is easy enough for every day but tasty enough for company. It may be made ahead and reheated in the oven or on the stove prior to serving.

Apple Pecan Quinoa

Instructions:

1. Using a box grater or food processor, shred 2 of the apples.

2. Bring quinoa and milk to a simmer in a medium saucepan, stirring often. Stir in grated apples, applesauce, sugar, cinnamon, and salt. Return to a simmer. Cover and cook on low for 25 minutes.

3. Chop remaining 2 apples. Stir in chopped apples and vanilla and re-cover. Cook for 5 to 10 more minutes. Remove from heat and let sit covered for 5 more minutes.

4. Divide among 4 serving bowls and top each with a tablespoon of pecans. If desired, drizzle with maple syrup. Serve warm. May be made ahead and reheated prior to serving.

4 apples, divided
1 cup quinoa, rinsed
1 ¼ cups milk or almond milk
¼ cup applesauce
3 tablespoons coconut palm sugar
1 teaspoon ground cinnamon
½ teaspoon sea salt
1 teaspoon vanilla extract
¼ cup chopped pecans
Optional: Maple syrup, for drizzling

Servings 4, Calories 346, Fat 8.7g, Carbohydrates 63.7g, Protein 7.1g, Cholesterol 0mg, Sodium 315mg, Fiber 8.6g, Sugars 27.6g

These gluten-free pancakes hit the spot when you need a little something special for breakfast!

Gluten-Free Quinoa Pancakes

Instructions:

1. If using flax egg, combine 2 tablespoons ground flax seeds and 6 tablespoons of water. Stir well and set aside. (Skip this step if you are using eggs.)

2. Coat a griddle or skillet with cooking spray and heat to medium low or 350 to 375 degrees.

3. Sift flour blend, baking powder, baking soda, and sea salt.

4. In a separate bowl combine almond milk, lemon juice, eggs or flax eggs, sweetener, melted coconut oil, and vanilla extract.

5. Combine wet ingredients with the sifted flour and stir until combined. Add quinoa and mix well. Add more milk one tablespoon at a time if a thinner pancake is desired.

6. Drop batter onto griddle using ¼-cup measure. Cook until the bottom is golden brown and the air bubbles start to pop. Flip and cook 3 to 5 minutes longer.

1 ⅔ cup all purpose gluten-free quinoa flour blend (see p. 30)
2 teaspoons baking powder
1 teaspoon baking soda
¾ teaspoon sea salt
1 ¾ cups milk or almond milk
2 teaspoons lemon juice
2 eggs or flax eggs
(2 tablespoons ground flax seeds + 6 tablespoons warm water)
1 tablespoon coconut nectar, maple syrup, or agave
1 tablespoon melted coconut oil
1 teaspoon vanilla extract
1 cup cooked quinoa

Servings 6, Calories 243, Fat 6.9g, Carbohydrates 37.2g, Protein 8.5g, Cholesterol 55 mg, Sodium 521mg, Fiber 4.9g, Sugars 2.7g

This is one of my favorite ways to start the day!

Coconut Oatmeal & Quinoa

Instructions:

Combine oatmeal, milk, and salt in a small saucepan. Bring to a boil. Reduce heat to low and add in quinoa, maple syrup and cranberries. Cook until the desired consistency. Top with walnuts and coconut and serve warm.

¼ cup oatmeal

1 ½ cups almond milk or milk of choice

1 pinch of salt

½ cup cooked quinoa

1 tablespoon maple syrup

1 tablespoon dried cranberries

1 tablespoon shredded coconut

1 tablespoon walnuts, chopped

Servings 1, Calories 350, Fat 14.4g, Carbohydrates 48.5g, Protein 9.8g, Cholesterol 0mg, Sodium 431mg, Fiber 8.1g, Sugars 12.7g

We've all been hearing for years how a healthy breakfast is the most important meal of the day, but that doesn't help when you are running short on time. This overnight muesli is a great solution. I've even prepped this ahead of time, including the berries, almonds, and syrup, and taken it on the road!

Creamy Overnight Quinoa Muesli

Instructions:

1. Core the apple and grate using a box grater or food processor. Place in a small bowl and add quinoa flakes, cooked quinoa, flax seeds, chia seeds, water, yogurt, and dried berries. Stir until well combined and refrigerate overnight.

2. Place muesli into 2 bowls and top with berries and almonds. Drizzle each bowl with a tablespoon of maple syrup and serve.

1 apple
½ cup quinoa flakes
½ cup cooked quinoa (or oatmeal)
1 tablespoon flax seeds
1 tablespoon chia seeds
1 cup water
1 cup vanilla or mixed berry yogurt—soy, coconut, or dairy
½ cup dried cranberries, cherries or strawberries
½ cup fresh berries
1 tablespoon slivered almonds
2 tablespoons maple syrup

Servings 2, Calories 418, Fat 8.2g, Carbohydrates 70.8g, Protein 15.5g, Cholesterol 7mg, Sodium 96mg, Fiber 10g, Sugars 35g

I am generally home to make breakfast, but on the days I am on the run, this is one of my go-to smoothies! If you are allergic to peanut butter, try almond butter or sun butter.

Peanut Butter Banana Smoothie

Instructions:

Place all ingredients in a blender and process until smooth. Add ice if desired.

2 tablespoons quinoa flakes

1 cup almond milk

½ banana, peeled and sliced

1 tablespoon natural peanut butter

1 scoop protein powder* (optional)

Stevia, to taste (optional)

*Note: nutritional information uses Garden of Life Raw Protein with 90 calories.
Servings 1, Calories 332, Fat 12.4g, Carbohydrates 34.2g, Protein 25.3g, Cholesterol 0mg, Sodium 184mg, Fiber 10.4g, Sugars 9g,

My boys declared these gluten-free pancakes the "best ever." Neither one is gluten intolerant so that is a huge complement!

Pumpkin Pancakes

Instructions:

1. If using flax egg combine 2 tablespoons ground flax seeds and 6 tablespoons of water. Stir well and set aside.

2. Coat a griddle or skillet with cooking spray and heat to medium low or 350 to 375 degrees.

3. Sift together flour blend, baking powder, baking soda, cinnamon, ginger, and sea salt.

4. In a separate bowl combine almond milk, pumpkin puree, lemon juice, eggs or flax eggs, sweetener, melted coconut oil, and vanilla extract.

5. Combine wet ingredients with the sifted flour and stir until combined. Add quinoa and mix well. Add more milk one tablespoon at a time if a thinner pancake is desired.

6. Drop batter onto griddle using ¼-cup measure. Cook until the bottom is golden brown and the air bubbles start to pop. Flip and cook 3 to 5 minutes longer.

2 cups all purpose gluten-free
   quinoa flour blend (see p. 30)
2 teaspoons baking powder
1 teaspoon baking soda
1 teaspoon cinnamon
½ teaspoon ground ginger
¾ teaspoon sea salt
1 ¾ cup milk or almond milk
¾ cup pumpkin puree
2 teaspoons lemon juice
2 eggs or flax eggs
   (2 tablespoons ground flax
   seeds + 6 tablespoons
   warm water)
1 tablespoon coconut nectar,
   maple syrup or agave
1 tablespoon melted
   coconut oil
1 teaspoon vanilla extract
1 cup cooked quinoa

Servings 6, Calories 306, Fat 5.5g, Carbohydrates 55.2g, Protein 7.4g, Cholesterol 55mg, Sodium 521mg, Fiber 2.1g, Sugars 3.5g

This is one sure-fire way I can get my boys to eat quinoa and oats for breakfast. My youngest son prefers it drier, with just 2 cups of milk. I, on the other hand, like a moister casserole and prefer to use 3 cups. You can adjust the moisture to suit your taste.

Pumpkin Quinoa Breakfast Casserole

Instructions:

1. Preheat oven to 350 degrees. Spray a medium casserole pan with olive oil.

2. In a medium bowl mix together oats, quinoa, walnuts, cranberries, chia seeds, baking powder, cinnamon, and sea salt. Spread mixture evenly in prepared pan.

3. If using flax egg, mix together 1 tablespoon ground flax seeds with 3 tablespoons warm water. Set aside to thicken. (Skip this step if you are using eggs.)

4. In a separate bowl mix together (flax) egg, maple syrup, pumpkin puree, milk, coconut oil, and vanilla extract. Pour mixture over quinoa oat mixture, ensuring that oats are fully covered.

5. Bake for 35 minutes.

6. Meanwhile, make streusel topping by combining flour, oats, walnuts, palm sugar, and butter in a small bowl.

7. Remove casserole from oven and top with streusel topping. Return to oven and bake for 15 minutes longer. Serve warm with an additional pat of butter or drizzle of maple syrup if desired.

Servings 12, Calories 388, Fat 25.2g, Carbohydrates 35.8g, Protein 8.4g, Cholesterol 26mg, Sodium 137mg, Fiber 5.5g, Sugars 10.1g

1 cup gluten-free rolled oats
1 cup quinoa, rinsed
½ cup toasted walnuts
¾ cup dried cranberries
2 tablespoon chia seeds (optional)
1 teaspoon baking powder
1 teaspoon ground cinnamon
½ teaspoon sea salt
1 large egg or flax egg
  (1 tablespoon ground flax seeds +3 tablespoons warm water)
⅓ cup maple syrup
⅔ cup pumpkin puree
2–3 cups almond milk (or milk of choice)
3 tablespoons coconut oil, melted and slightly cooled
2 teaspoons vanilla extract

Streusel Topping
⅔ cup toasted quinoa flour (or gluten-free flour of choice)
1 cup gluten-free oats
⅓ cup chopped walnuts,
3 tablespoons coconut palm sugar
4 tablespoons softened Earth Balance or butter

Starting the day with chocolate always seems a little decadent to me—even when it is healthy!

Chocolate Quinoa Porridge

Instructions:

1. Bring quinoa flakes or quinoa, cocoa powder, and water or milk to a simmer in a medium saucepan. Reduce heat and simmer for about 7 minutes, or until most of the liquid has absorbed. Stir occasionally to prevent sticking.

2. Add vanilla, dried cherries, sunflower seeds, and maple syrup and stir until heated through. Transfer to a serving bowl and garnish with cocoa nibs and strawberries.

⅓ cup quinoa flakes or cooked quinoa

½ tablespoon cocoa powder or cacao powder

¾ cup water or milk of choice

1 teaspoon vanilla

1 tablespoon dried cherries

1 tablespoon sunflower seeds

1 tablespoon maple syrup

½ tablespoon cocoa nibs or chocolate chips

½ cup sliced strawberries

Servings 12, Calories 388, Fat 25.2g, Carbohydrates 35.8g, Protein 8.4g, Cholesterol 26mg, Sodium 137mg, Fiber 5.5g, Sugars 10.1g

Appetizers & Snacks

These zucchini chips are so crunchy that no one knew they were baked not fried!

Quinoa Baked Zucchini Chips with Sriracha Dipping Sauce

Instructions:

1. Preheat oven to 425 degrees. Place a wire rack on top of a baking sheet.

2. Combine almond milk and lemon juice and set aside.

3. Place quinoa flour, quinoa flakes, rice crackers, garlic powder, onion powder, smoked paprika, sea salt, and black pepper in a food processor. Pulse until smooth.

4. Dredge zucchini wedges in quinoa and cracker mixture (only a little bit will stick). Dip in milk mixture and then recoat with the quinoa mixture. Spray or brush with olive oil. Place on wire rack and bake for 20 to 25 minutes, until golden brown. If desired, serve with Siraracha Dipping Sauce

5. Sriracha Dipping Sauce: Combine all ingredients in a small bowl and mix until well combined. Store in the refrigerator until chilled.

1 large zucchini, sliced into ¼-inch thick rounds
⅔ cup almond milk (or milk of choice)
1 tablespoon lemon juice
½ cup toasted quinoa flour
¾ cup quinoa flakes
½ cup crumbled rice crackers
1 teaspoon garlic powder
1 teaspoon onion powder
1 teaspoon smoked paprika
½ teaspoon sea salt
½ teaspoon fresh cracked black pepper
Olive oil spray

Sriracha Dipping Sauce

⅓ cup tofu mayo or Greek Yogurt
1–3 teaspoons Sriracha (to taste)
1 tablespoon fresh lime juice
3 cloves minced garlic

Dipping Sauce: Servings 6, Calories 12, Fat 0, Carbohydrates 1.2g, Protein 1.9g, Cholesterol 0mg, Sodium 7mg, Sugars 0.6g

Servings 6, Calories 212, Fat 8.3g, Carbohydrates 29g, Protein 6.3g, Cholesterol 1mg, Sodium 173mg, Fiber 3.1g, Sugars 3.7g

I love granola bars for when we travel or for when I know that the boys and I will be out for most of the day.

Apple Granola Bars

Instructions:

1. Preheat oven to 350 degrees. Combine quinoa flakes, oats, almonds, and sunflower seeds and place on a rimmed, parchment-lined baking sheet. Bake for 15 minutes, stirring half way through.

2. Move to a large bowl and stir in quinoa flour, flax seeds, dried apples and coconut.

3. If using chia egg in place of egg, mix chia seeds with warm water and set aside until a gel forms.

4. Meanwhile, melt almond butter and coconut oil in a medium saucepan. Stir in honey and applesauce and cook on medium for 2 minutes. Stir in chia mixture OR egg, vanilla, cinnamon, and sea salt.

5. Prepare baking sheet by covering it with parchment paper and spraying the parchment lightly with cooking spray. Press quinoa/oat mixture into baking sheet and bake for 15 to 18 minutes, until edges are brown. Cool on a wire rack and cut into bars. Store in an airtight container.

2 cups quinoa flakes

1 cup gluten-free oats

1 cup almonds, chopped

½ cup raw sunflower seeds

1 egg or chia egg
  (1 tablespoon chia seeds +
   3 tablespoons warm water)

½ cup toasted quinoa flour

¼ cup ground flax seeds

½ cup dried apples, chopped

½ cup coconut flakes

½ cup almond butter

⅔ cup coconut oil

⅔ cup honey or agave nectar

½ cup applesauce

2 teaspoons vanilla extract

1 teaspoon ground cinnamon

¼ teaspoon sea salt

Servings 18, Calories 302, Fat 18.9g, Carbohydrates 29.2g, Protein 6.1g, Cholesterol 0mg, Sodium 31mg, Fiber 4.3g, Sugars 12.7g

Quinoa Chickpea Crackers

Instructions:

1. Preheat oven to 350 degrees. Line 2 baking sheets with parchment paper.

2. In a blender or food processor, pulse chickpeas and quinoa until smooth. Add in salt, pepper, gluten-free flour blend, xanthan gum, vegetable shortening, and nutritional yeast. With machine running, add in 3 tablespoons of water until a dough forms.

3. Roll dough out to ⅛ inch thickness. Brush with almond milk and cut into rectangles. Place on prepared baking sheet and sprinkle with sesame seeds and sea salt.

4. Bake for 30 to 35 minutes. Allow to cool on baking sheets then store in an airtight container.

1 cup chickpeas, drained and rinsed

½ cup cooked quinoa

1 teaspoon sea salt

½ teaspoon fresh ground pepper

1½ cups all purpose gluten-free flour blend

½ teaspoon xanthan gum

5 tablespoons cold vegetable shortening (like spectrum organics)

2 tablespoons nutritional yeast

2 tablespoons unsweetened almond milk or milk of choice

1½ tablespoons sesame seeds

1½ tablespoons coarse sea salt

Servings 12, Calories 160, Fat 6.3g, Carbohydrates 21.8g, Protein 3.6g, Cholesterol 0mg, Sodium 916mg, Fiber 7g, Sugars 1g

These little pizzettes can be prepped up to 2 hours ahead of time and baked just before serving!

Tomato & Olive Pizzettes with Quinoa Crust

Instructions:

1. Place pizza stone on the bottom rack of the oven and preheat oven to 425 degrees.

2. On a large sheet of parchment paper, roll out dough until it is between ¼ to ⅛ inch thick. Using a round 3-inch cookie cutter, cut the dough into 15 rounds.

3. Transfer rounds to a pizza peel lined with parchment paper. Brush with ½ tablespoon olive oil and sprinkle with salt and pepper. Brush on top of rounds and top with tapenade.

4. In a medium bowl combine cherry tomatoes, remaining olive oil, fennel seeds, and red pepper flakes. Place on top of the pizza rounds and top with crumbled cheese or dollops of cream cheese. Sprinkle the rounds with fresh oregano.

5. Carefully transfer parchment paper to pizza stone and cook for 20 minutes.

1 pound quinoa pizza dough (see p. 105)

1½ tablespoons olive oil, divided

½ teaspoon salt

¼ teaspoon fresh ground pepper

3 tablespoons olive tapenade

1 cup grape tomatoes, quartered

1 teaspoon fennel seeds

⅛ to ¼ teaspoon crushed red pepper flakes

2 ounces goat cheese or vegan cream cheese

2 teaspoons chopped fresh oregano

{ Servings 12, Calories 137, Fat 6.5g, Carbohydrates 17.1g, Protein 4.3g, Cholesterol 5mg, Sodium 305mg, Fiber 1.7g }

As a child some of my happiest memories were cuddled up with my mother watching movies and TV specials. As a working mom, she was often tired and frequently stressed, but in these moments she was always an excited child again. Now that I'm the mom, I cherish these moments with my boys even more. And I always try to make them even more memorable with a special snack! I can only hope that one day they will continue the tradition with their children—and that I will be around to be part of it.

Quinoa Cashew Crunch 'n' Munch

Instructions:

1. In a large heavy saucepan, bring agave nectar, butter, almond butter, sugar, sea salt, and water to a boil, stirring often. Remove from heat and stir in popcorn, cashews, apples, and quinoa.

2. Arrange mixture on rimmed baking sheets lined with parchment paper. Allow to set for at least 20 minutes.

⅓ cup agave nectar, coconut nectar, or maple syrup
2 tablespoons Earth Balance or butter
⅓ cup almond butter
½ cup coconut palm sugar
1 teaspoon sea salt
2 tablespoons water
10 cups popped popcorn
1 cup chopped cashews
½ cup chopped dried apples
1 cup popped quinoa*

*Note:

To Pop Quinoa: Place coconut oil in a popcorn popper and allow to get warm. Add quinoa and cook about 5 minutes, until quinoa is lightly brown. Alternatively, pop the quinoa in a covered saucepan, shaking to prevent burning.

Servings 12, Calories 257, Fat 12.4g, Carbohydrates 33.5g, Protein 5.6g, Cholesterol 5mg, Sodium 192mg, Fiber 2.6g, Sugars 12.3g

The first time I made this recipe my oh-so-skeptical family was blown away. I was seriously worried about there being any left to photograph as I put the last ones together!

Quinoa Spring Rolls with Spicy Peanut Sauce

Instructions:

1. Working one at a time, soak wrappers in a large bowl of hot water for a few seconds and then transfer to a clean, dry work surface.

2. Place the quinoa across the right 1/3 of each wrapper. Top with lettuce, carrots, sprouts, cabbage, cilantro, and basil. Add a tablespoon of sauce and sesame seeds and roll the wrapper tightly over the filling, tucking the ends in as you roll. Cover with a lightly damp towel as you continue to make your rolls. When ready to serve, cut in half and serve with additional sauce.

3. To make sauce, combine all ingredients in a blender or food processor and process until smooth. Adjust seasonings to taste.

Nutritional Info for Spring Rolls: Calories 166, Fat 5.2g, Carbohydrates 22g, Protein 5.7g, Cholesterol 0 mg, Sodium 19 mg, Fiber 3.2g, Sugars 1.8g

Peanut Dipping Sauce (1/5 of recipe): Calories 182, Fat 13.1g, Carbohydrates 8g, Protein 9.3g, Fiber 2.1g, Sugar 2.3g

10 spring roll rice paper wrappers

2 cups cooked quinoa

½ cup julienned carrots

½ cup sprouts

1 cup napa cabbage, chopped

2 cups lettuce, chopped

¼ cup chopped cilantro

½ cup chopped basil

¼ cup sesame seeds, toasted

Peanut Dipping Sauce

½ cup natural peanut butter

¼ cup hot water

2 tablespoons of gluten-free tamari sauce

2 tablespoons lime juice

2 tablespoons seasoned rice vinegar

2 teaspoons tomato paste or ketchup

2 cloves garlic, minced

2 teaspoons white miso, optional

1 tablespoon fresh ginger, minced

½ teaspoon crushed red pepper flakes

This is a great breakfast for those days where you just don't have time to sit down and eat!

Quinoa Power Bars

Instructions:

1. Preheat oven to 350 degrees. Line a rimmed baking sheet with parchment paper. Toss the quinoa flakes, cashews, and sunflower seeds and toast for 25 to 30 minutes, stirring occasionally.

2. Place in a large bowl and allow to cool slightly. Add in flax seeds, chia seeds, dried cherries, and chocolate chips.

3. In a small saucepan melt coconut oil. Add almond butter, applesauce, and maple syrup. Bring to a boil and lower heat to medium low. Cook for 3 minutes and stir in vanilla and sea salt. Pour mixture over dry ingredients.

4. Transfer mixture to a rimmed baking sheet lined with parchment paper and press into a rectangle. Bake for 10 minutes. Allow to cool and then place into refrigerator until firm. Cut into desired shape. Drizzle with chocolate if desired.

2 cups quinoa flakes

1 cup chopped cashews

½ cup raw sunflower seeds

⅓ cup ground flax seeds

⅓ cup chia seeds

¾ cup dried cherries, chopped

½ cup carob or chocolate chips

2 tablespoons coconut oil

2 tablespoons almond butter

½ cup unsweetened applesauce

⅔ cup maple syrup

2 teaspoons vanilla extract

½ teaspoon sea salt

Optional: melted chocolate, for drizzling

{ Servings 12, Calories 309, Fat 15.9g, Carbohydrates 35.3g, Protein 8g, Cholesterol 0mg, Sodium 101mg, Fiber 6.8g, Sugars 15.8g }

This is one of my favorite uses for my multi-purpose pizza dough!

Gluten-Free Cinnamon Bites

Instructions:

1. Preheat oven to 425 degrees. Line a large baking sheet with parchment paper.

2. Place another large piece of parchment paper on your counter and sprinkle with gluten-free flour. Roll crust into a rectangle, sprinkling with additional flour as necessary to prevent sticking.

3. Using a pastry brush, spread butter evenly on the crust. Combine cinnamon and sugar in a small bowl and sprinkle on top.

4. Starting at the long side of the dough, use your hands to gently roll the dough tightly. (You will be forming a long log.) Cut the dough with a sharp knife or kitchen shears into small bites.

5. Place on a parchment-lined baking sheet and bake for 20 to 25 minutes, until golden brown. Store for 2 days at room temperature or 1 week in the refrigerator.

1 lb quinoa pizza dough (see p. 105)
3 tablespoons butter or Earth Balance
¼ cup brown sugar or coconut palm sugar
½ tablespoon cinnamon

Servings 12, Calories 117, Fat 4.2g, Carbohydrates 19.1g, Protein 2.7g, Cholesterol 8mg, Sodium 180mg, Fiber 1.5g, Sugars 2.9g

This is a great appetizer that never fails to please!

Veggie Quinoa Pizza Roll

Instructions:

1. Place a pizza stone on the bottom rack of the oven and preheat to 425 degrees.

2. Heat a large skillet to medium and add onion. Cook for 8 minutes. Add spinach or kale and cook until wilted. Add garlic and cook for 1 more minute. Transfer to a medium bowl and toss with roasted red peppers.

3. Roll pizza crust into a large rectangle on a sheet of parchment paper, using gluten-free flour as needed to avoid sticking. Spread vegetable mixture evenly, leaving a 1-inch border. Top with mozzarella and ½ of the Parmesan and sprinkle with oregano and red chili flakes.

4. Fold the short ends of the dough in and roll the long end, using the parchment paper as needed to assist in rolling. Sprinkle with remaining Parmesan. Use a pizza peel or back of a cookie sheet, transfer parchment paper to your pizza stone.

5. Bake for 25 to 30 minutes, or until golden brown. Serve warm with marinara for dipping.

1 pound quinoa pizza dough (see p. 105)

(see p. 105)

1 red onion, diced

4 ounces fresh spinach or kale

3 cloves garlic minced

2 roasted red peppers, chopped

6 ounces fresh mozzarella cheese, crumbled or Daiya mozzarella

3 ounces Parmesan cheese or vegan Parmesan substituted

1 tablespoon fresh oregano, chopped

¼ teaspoon red chili flakes

Marinara, for serving

Servings 12, Calories 156, Fat 5.4g, Carbohydrates 18.7g, Protein 10.3g, Cholesterol 6mg, Sodium 365mg, Fiber 2g, Sugars 1.1g

I like to serve this with a little Greek yogurt mixed with a chipotle chili, lime juice, and garlic!

Quinoa Taquitos

Instructions:

1. Cook bacon according to package directions. Drain on paper towels.

2. In a medium bowl stir bacon, quinoa, cream cheese, chipotle chili, lime juice, garlic, taco seasoning, nutritional yeast, cilantro, and green onions.

3. Heat the tortillas in a warm skillet until pliable.

4. Spoon quinoa mixture into tortillas and secure with 2 toothpicks.

5. Heat oil in a large skillet over medium heat. Cook until brown on all sides, flipping as necessary. (Alternatively, you can bake at 425 degrees for 10 minutes, flip and cook an additional 5–10 minutes.)

8 ounces tempeh bacon or turkey bacon (optional)*
2 cups cooked quinoa
4 ounces cream cheese or vegan cream cheese substitute, softened
1 chipotle chili in adobo sauce, chopped fine
2 tablespoons lime juice
3 cloves garlic
1 tablespoon taco seasoning
2 tablespoons nutritional yeast (optional)
¼ cup fresh cilantro, chopped
¼ cup red onion, chopped
8 corn tortillas
coconut oil, for cooking
For serving: Greek yogurt, sour cream, or guacamole

*Please note that most commercially available tempeh bacon does contain gluten, so if you are vegan or vegetarian you will need to make your own or omit this ingredient. I like to make my own—you can see the recipe I use here: http://kblog.lunchboxbunch.com/2009/06/tempeh-bacon-recipe-vegan-facon-makes.html.

Servings 8, Calories 223, Fat 9.3g, Carbohydrates 25.5 g, Protein 10.6g, Cholesterol 16 mg, Sodium 58 mg, Fiber 5.5g

I love this served with both marinara and ranch!

Quinoa Polenta Wedges

Instructions:

1. Line a 13 x 9 pan with parchment paper and spray with olive oil.

2. Heat a small skillet to medium heat and spray with olive oil. Add onion and sun dried tomatoes and cook for 10 to 12 minutes, until tender. Add minced garlic and cook for 1 more minute.

3. Bring water to boil in a large saucepan. Add polenta in a steady stream and whisk well to combine. Continue to stir for about 3 minutes. Add in quinoa, milk, onion, salt, pepper, cayenne, smoked paprika, and nutritional yeast. Stir until the liquid has absorbed and the mixture has thickened. Add in fresh chives and cheese and cook for 1 more minute. Taste and add more salt and pepper as desired.

4. Spoon mixture into prepared pan and smooth the top, using a spoon dipped in cold water if necessary. Cover and refrigerate for 2 hours. Remove polenta from pan and cut into squares. Cut each square in half diagonally to form triangles.

5. Pan fry: Heat oil in a pan over medium heat. Cook for 4 to 5 minutes per side.

6. Broil: Spray triangles with oil and broil for 7 minutes. Flip and cook 8 more minutes.

7. Grill: Spray triangles with olive oil and grill until seared on both sides.

8. Serve with marinara, ranch dressing, or a roasted red pepper dip if desired.

olive oil spray

1 onion, chopped

½ cup sun dried tomatoes, chopped and rehydrated

4 cloves garlic, minced

4¼ cups water

1½ cups coarse cornmeal or polenta

1½ cups cooked quinoa

½ cup milk of choice

1 teaspoon salt

½ teaspoon fresh ground pepper

¼ teaspoon cayenne pepper

1 teaspoon smoked paprika

3 tablespoons nutritional yeast (optional)

¼ cup fresh chives, parsley, rosemary, or thyme

½ cup grated mozzarella or Daiya shreds

For serving: marinara, ranch dressing, roasted red pepper dip

Servings 6, Calories 254, Fat 4.8g, Carbohydrates 45.8g, Protein 7.7g, Cholesterol 0mg, Sodium 531mg, Fiber 4.3g, Sugars 1.2g

Baking

Think you are relegated to a life of eating dense bread purchased in the freezer section? One bite of this loaf will have you convinced that gluten-free bread does not have to be inferior to its wheat counterpart.

Quinoa Bread

Instructions:

1. Lightly grease a 9 x 5 loaf pan.

2. If using flax eggs in place of eggs, combine 2 tablespoons ground flax seeds with 6 tablespoons warm water. Mix well and set aside. (Skip this step if you are using eggs.)

3. In a small bowl combine warm water and honey or maple syrup. Sprinkle yeast on top and stir gently. Set aside for 5 to 10 minutes, until it begins to foam.

4. In a large mixing bowl, combine quinoa flour, tapioca starch, corn starch, milk powder, xanthan gum, and sea salt. In a separate bowl combine yeast mixture, beaten eggs and oil. Add wet mixture to the dry ingredients and beat for 3 minutes at medium speed.

5. Transfer to the prepared pan and use a spoon dipped in cold water to smooth the top. If desired, sprinkle with sesame seeds. Cover with a damp cloth and allow to rise for 1 hour.

6. Place a small pan on the bottom rack of your oven. Preheat oven to 350 degrees. Add 1 cup of water to the pan in the bottom of your oven and then place the loaf in the oven. Bake for 40 to 45 minutes. Allow to cool in the pan for 5 minutes and then turn out into a wire cooling rack. Best stored in the refrigerator.

1½ cups warm water, 105–110 degrees
2½ tablespoons honey or maple syrup
2¼ teaspoons active dry yeast
1¼ cups toasted quinoa flour
1 cup tapioca starch
1 cup cornstarch
2 tablespoons dry milk powder or rice milk powder
3 teaspoons xanthan gum
1¾ teaspoons fine sea salt
2 eggs lightly beaten or flax eggs (2 tablespoons ground flax seeds + 6 tablespoons warm water)
2 tablespoons melted coconut, canola or olive oil
Sesame seeds, optional

Servings 18, Calories 127, Carbohydrates 23g, Protein 2.2g, Cholesterol 18mg, Sodium 196mg, Fiber .9g, Fat 2.2g, Sugars 3.3g

This rich but absolutely delicious recipe makes 8 full-sized scones. If you are serving them as part of a holiday buffet, you will want to cut them into 16 pieces rather than 8!

Cranberry Quinoa Scones

Instructions:

1. Preheat oven to 400 degrees. Line a baking sheet with parchment paper.

2. In a small bowl, combine almond milk and lemon juice. Set aside to curdle.

3. In a large bowl sift together brown rice flour, sorghum flour, quinoa flour, potato starch, tapioca starch, xanthan gum, sugar, baking powder, baking soda, and salt. Stir in orange peel. Using fingers or a pastry cutter, mix in butter until you have a coarse meal. Stir in cranberries.

4. Mix in milk mixture, ¼ cup at a time, mixing with a fork as you go. Place mixture on a sheet of parchment paper and knead briefly. Form into a round, about an inch thick. Cut into 8 pieces.

5. Transfer pieces to parchment-lined baking sheet. Bake for about 25 minutes. Remove from oven and allow to sit on the baking sheet for another 10 minutes. Serve warm.

1 cup chilled almond milk (or milk of choice)
1 tablespoon lemon juice
1 cup extra fine brown rice flour
¾ cup sorghum flour
½ cup toasted quinoa flour
½ cup potato starch
¼ cup tapioca starch
1 ½ teaspoons xanthan gum
⅓ cup coconut palm sugar
3 teaspoons baking powder
½ teaspoon baking soda
1 ¼ teaspoons kosher salt
1 tablespoon grated orange peel
¾ cup chilled Earth Balance or unsalted butter
¾ cup dried cranberries

Note: Toasting quinoa flour brings out its nutty flavor, and helps eliminate the strong odor. To toast it, line a rimmed baking sheet with parchment paper. Spread quinoa flour to no more than ¼ inch thick. Place in a 220 degree oven and toast for 90 minutes. Store in an airtight container in the refrigerator or freezer.

Servings 8, Calories 342, Fat 18.6g, Carbohydrates 42.9g, Protein 3.7g, Cholesterol 0mg, Sodium 667mg, Fiber 2.9g, Sugars 7.3g

This is one of those breads I have to make only when I know company is coming. Otherwise, I'll end up eating the entire loaf myself!

Apple Onion Focaccia Bread

Instructions:

1. Coat an 8 x 8 baking pan with olive oil and then dust with cornmeal. (If you are allergic to corn use flour.)

2. In a small bowl combine warm water, coconut palm sugar, and yeast. Stir gently to combine and allow to sit for 5 to 10 minutes, or until yeast froths.

3. In the bowl of a stand mixer combine flour, salt, and yeast. Mix on low until the dough comes together, then increase the speed to medium. Add olive oil and mix for 3 to 5 minutes.

4. Transfer to prepared pan and spray the top with olive oil. Cover with a moist towel and allow to rise in a warm place for an hour.

5. Meanwhile, heat olive oil to medium in a skillet. Add onion and cook for 8 to 10 minutes. Reduce heat to low and cook for another 20 minutes. Add apples to the pan and cook for 10 minutes longer.

6. Preheat oven to 425 degrees. Dimple dough with your fingertips. Brush with olive oil and then top with onion and apple mixture. Sprinkle with rosemary and bake for 20 to 25 minutes. Serve warm.

Cornmeal, for dusting
1½ cups warm water (105–115 degrees)
½ tablespoon coconut palm sugar
2¼ teaspoons rapid rise yeast
3 cups gluten-free all purpose quinoa flour blend (see p. 30)
1 tablespoon sea salt
¼ cup olive oil

Topping

2 tablespoons olive oil
1 sweet onion, diced
½ tart cooking apple, cored and sliced thin
1 tablespoon fresh rosemary or 1 teaspoon dried

Servings 12, Calories 215, Fat 6.6g, Carbohydrates 34.9g, Protein 3.1g, Cholesterol 0mg, Sodium 471mg, Fiber .6g, Sugars 1.6g

Quinoa English Muffins

Instructions:

1. In a medium bowl combine water, maple syrup and yeast. Set aside to proof for 5 to 10 minutes.

2. In the bowl to your stand mixer, combine flour blend, xanthan gum, and sea salt. Mix well with a wire whisk. Add cooked quinoa and stir to combine.

3. Line two baking sheets with parchment paper. Spray 12 English muffin rings with olive oil spray or coat with vegetable shortening. Don't be stingy with the oil or your muffins may stick! Place prepared muffin rings on the parchment-lined baking sheets.

4. Preheat oven to proof setting or 175 degrees.

5. When the yeast mixture is frothy, add it, the coconut oil, apple cider vinegar, and remaining water to the dry ingredients.

6. Fit your stand mixer with a paddle attachment and blend on medium high for 3 minutes. The dough will be wet and spreadable.

7. Using a ⅓-cup measure scoop dough into prepared muffin rings. Using a cool wet spoon, smooth the tops. Place the baking sheet in the oven and allow to rise for 15 minutes.

8. Remove from oven and preheat oven to 425 degrees. Bake for 35 minutes, rotating trays half way through. Check during the last 10 minutes and cover with foil to prevent over browning.

9. Cool on the tray for 15 minutes and then remove muffins from rings and allow to cool completely.

10. Muffins may be frozen.

Servings 12, Calories 227, Fat 6.5g, Carbohydrates 37.3g, Protein 3.5g, Cholesterol 0mg, Sodium 353mg, Fiber 1.1g, Sugars 2.0g

Wet Ingredients

2 cups warm water (105–110 degrees)

2 tablespoons maple syrup or honey

½ tablespoon active dry yeast

⅓ cup melted coconut oil

½ tablespoon raw apple cider vinegar

¼ cup warm water

Dry Ingredients

3 cups all purpose gluten-free quinoa flour blend (see p. 30)

1 teaspoon xanthan gum

¾ tablespoon sea salt

1 cup cooked quinoa

These muffins are a favorite with my boys! I've even iced them for special-occasion cupcakes.

Chocolate Chip Quinoa Muffins

Instructions:

1. Preheat oven to 350 degrees. Line a 12-cup muffin tin with paper baking cups. Spray lightly with olive oil spray.

2. If using flax eggs, combine 2 tablespoons ground flax seeds plus 6 tablespoons warm water. (Skip this step if you are using eggs.)

3. In a large bowl, sift together self-rising flour, quinoa flour, baking powder, and sea salt. Stir in cooked quinoa.

4. In a separate bowl whisk together coconut palm sugar, maple syrup, apple sauce, melted coconut oil, milk, yogurt, (flax) eggs, and vanilla extract. Add wet ingredient to the dry ingredients and stir until just combined. Stir in chocolate chips.

5. Using a measuring spoon or ice cream scoop, fill the muffin cups. Bake until golden brown, about 30 to 35 minutes. Let cool in the pan on a rack for 20 minutes. Separate tops with a knife if necessary. Invert and remove muffins from the pan.

3 cups gluten-free all purpose quinoa flour blend (see p. 30)

1 teaspoon baking powder

½ teaspoon sea salt

1 cup cooked quinoa

1 cup coconut palm sugar

⅓ cup maple syrup or agave nectar

½ cup applesauce

3 tablespoons coconut oil, melted

1 cup milk of choice, at room temperature

1 cup soy or low fat plain yogurt

2 room temperature eggs or flax eggs (2 tablespoons flax eggs + 6 tablespoons warm water)

1½ teaspoon vanilla extract

1 cup chocolate chips

Servings 12, Calories 356, Fat 7.6g, Carbohydrates 66.5g, Protein 6.2g, Cholesterol 29mg, Sodium 155mg, Fiber .5g, Sugars 25.1g

My favorite way to enjoy this bread is toasted with a pat of butter or Earth Balance. It also makes a rustic and filling sandwich.

Hearty Quinoa Bread

Instructions:

1. Prepare a 9 x 5 loaf pan by spraying with cooking spray.

2. In a small bowl combine honey and water. Sprinkle yeast on top and set aside for about 10 minutes, or until frothy.

3. If using flax eggs, combine 3 tablespoons ground flax seeds plus 9 tablespoons warm water in a small bowl. Stir well and set aside.

4. In a medium bowl mix together sorghum flour, quinoa flour, potato starch, tapioca starch, xanthan gum, and sea salt. Add in sunflower seeds, quinoa, and chia seeds and stir until well combined. In a large bowl or the bowl to your stand mixer combine (flax) eggs, milk, coconut oil, molasses, and vinegar. Add the flour mixture to the egg mixture and beat on low for about 1 ½ minutes. Add yeast and beat for 3 minutes at medium high. Pour the batter into the prepared loaf pan. Place in a warm location and cover with a moist towel. Allow to rise for 1 hour.

5. Preheat oven to 350 degrees. Bake loaf for 45 to 55 minutes, until the crust is a dark brown. Cool for 10 minutes in the pan and then turn out onto a cutting board.

{ Servings 16, Calories 164, Fat 7.9g, Carbohydrates 20.2g, Protein 4.6g, Cholesterol 31mg, Sodium 196mg, Fiber 2.9g, Sugars 4.3g }

1 tablespoon honey or maple syrup
¼ cup warm water (105–110 degrees)
2¼ teaspoons yeast
¾ cup sorghum flour
½ cup toasted quinoa flour
½ cup potato starch
¼ cup tapioca starch
1 tablespoon xanthan gum
1½ teaspoons sea salt
1 cup sunflower seeds
½ cup quinoa, rinsed
¼ cup chia seeds
3 eggs or flax eggs (3 tablespoons ground flax seeds PLUS 9 tablespoons warm water)
½ cup milk of choice
¼ cup melted coconut oil, cooled slightly or organic canola oil
¼ cup organic molasses
1½ tablespoons apple cider vinegar

Not only does this dough taste great, but it also freezes well. I love knowing that I have crusts in the freezer to pull out for busy weeknights.

Gluten-Free Flour Blend Pizza Dough

Instructions:

1. If using flax eggs, combine flax seeds with warm water and set aside.

2. In a small bowl combine yeast, 1 cup of the water, and 1 tablespoon of sugar. Mix well and set aside for 10 minutes until bubbly.

3. Meanwhile, in a large bowl combine remaining 1 tablespoon sugar, gluten-free flour blend, cornmeal, salt, and xanthan gum. Mix until combined. Add in quinoa, (flax) eggs, olive oil, remaining 2 ¼ cups water, and yeast mixture. Using a heavy stand mixer, mix well until your dough comes together. (You may also mix with a spoon; you may need to use your hands in the end.)

4. Spray a large bowl with olive oil and transfer dough. Cover with a cloth and allow to rise in a warm spot for 2 hours.

5. The dough can be used immediately, though I've found it is much easier to deal with cold. Refrigerate for 5 days or freeze for up to 3 weeks. If frozen, defrost in the refrigerator overnight prior to using.

6. When you are ready to cook, preheat oven to 425 and roll out on a parchment-lined pizza peel (the back of a large cookie sheet works, too). The dough is going to be moist and not have the pliability that a wheat crust would have. Add a little flour if you need to keep it from sticking to your rolling pin and roll out to ⅛ inch thick. Top with your favorite toppings. Transfer parchment paper to a pizza stone and cook for 10 minutes. Carefully slide parchment out from under crust. Cook for another 15 to 20 minutes, watching carefully toward the end.

2 eggs or flax eggs
2 tablespoons dry active yeast
3¼ cups lukewarm water
2 tablespoons coconut palm sugar or sugar of choice
4 cups gluten-free all purpose quinoa flour blend (see p. 30)
1½ cups cornmeal
1½ tablespoons sea salt
1 tablespoon xanthan gum
1½ cups cooked quinoa
½ cup olive oil

Makes 6 crusts

Servings 24, Calories 186, Fat 5.1g, Carbohydrates 30.6g, Protein 3.6g, Cholesterol 14mg, Sodium 11mg, Fiber 1.7g, Sugars .8g

My youngest son refuses to eat carrots, but loves these muffins. This is one of the best ways I've found to sneak them into his diet.

Cinnamon Carrot Muffins

Instructions:

1. Preheat oven to 350 degrees. Line a muffin tin with 9 paper cups. If using flax eggs, combine 2 tablespoons ground flax seeds with 6 tablespoons warm water. Whisk well and set aside.

2. In a large bowl combine gluten-free flour blend, cooked quinoa, coconut palm sugar, cinnamon, baking powder, baking soda and sea salt.

3. Combine milk and lemon juice in a small bowl. Set aside to curdle. If using flax eggs, combine 2 tablespoons ground flax seeds with 6 tablespoons warm water. Set aside to thicken.

4. In a medium bowl combine milk mixture, eggs or flax eggs and applesauce. Whisk until well combined. Add coconut oil and vanilla extract. Stir until combined and then add wet mixture to the dry mixture.

5. Stir in carrots until just combined and spoon batter into cups. Bake for 22 to 28 minutes, until a toothpick comes out clean.

6. Cool in pan for 10 minutes and then transfer to a wire rack to continue cooling. Top with cinnamon drizzle if desired.

7. To make cinnamon drizzle, combine all ingredients in a small bowl. Add additional milk until desired texture is achieved.

Muffins
Servings 9, Calories 221, Fat 9.4g, Carbohydrates 31.4g, Protein 3.4g, Cholesterol 36mg, Sodium 251mg, Fiber 1.2g, Sugars 10.4g

Optional Cinnamon Drizzle
Servings 9, Calories 28, Fat .2g, Carbohydrates 6.8g, Protein 0g, Cholesterol 0mg, Sodium 0mg, Sugars 6.6g

1 cup gluten-free all purpose quinoa flour blend (see p. 30)
½ cup cooked quinoa
½ cup coconut palm sugar
1 teaspoon ground cinnamon
2 teaspoons baking powder
1 teaspoon baking soda
¼ teaspoon sea salt
⅓ cup dairy or soy milk
1 teaspoon lemon juice
2 room-temperature eggs or flax eggs (2 tablespoons ground flax seeds + 6 tablespoons warm water)
¼ cup applesauce
⅓ cup coconut oil, melted
1 teaspoon vanilla extract
2 cups shredded carrots
Cinnamon drizzle, optional

Cinnamon Drizzle

½ cup powdered sugar
½ teaspoon cinnamon
½ tablespoon almond milk or milk of choice

This is my favorite multi-purpose pizza dough. I not only use it to make pizzas but also to make pizza rolls, garlic knots, and cinnamon bites! It freezes well so as a busy mom, this is one thing I try to always have on hand.

Quinoa Pizza Dough

Instructions:

1. If using flax eggs in place of eggs, combine ground flax seeds with 6 tablespoons warm water and set aside. (Skip this step if you are using eggs.)

2. In a large bowl combine flours, cornmeal, yeast, salt, and xanthan gum.

3. In a separate bowl combine liquid ingredients with the (flax) egg and sweetener. Add to the dry ingredients and mix well with a spoon or heavy duty stand mixer. (If you aren't using a machine you may need to use your hands.)

4. Cover with a cloth and allow to sit in a warm spot for 2 hours.

5. The dough can be used immediately, though I've found it is much easier to deal with cold. Refrigerate for 5 days or freeze for up to 3 weeks. If frozen, defrost in the refrigerator overnight prior to using.

6. When you are ready to cook, preheat oven to 425 degrees and roll out on a parchment-lined pizza peel (the back of a large cookie sheet works, too). The dough is going to be moist and not have the pliability that a wheat crust would have. Add a little flour if you need to keep it from sticking to your rolling pin and roll out to 1/8 inch thick. Top with your favorite toppings. Transfer parchment paper to a pizza stone and cook for 10 minutes. Carefully slide parchment out from under crust. Cook for another 15 to 20 minutes, watching carefully toward the end.

1 ½ cups sorghum flour

1 ½ cups toasted quinoa flour

1 cup millet flour

1 cup tapioca starch

1 cup potato starch

1 ½ cups corn flour

2 tablespoons dry active yeast

1 ½ tablespoons sea salt

2 tablespoons xanthan gum

2 eggs or 2 flax eggs
(2 tablespoons ground flax seeds + 6 tablespoons warm water)

3 ¼ cups lukewarm water

½ cup olive oil

2 tablespoons coconut palm sugar or sugar

Makes 5 one-pound crusts

Servings 20, Calories 237, Fat 7.1g, Carbohydrates 39.4g, Protein 4.8g, Cholesterol 16mg, Sodium 430mg, Fiber 3.2g, Sugars 1.9g

Although Masa Harina is a naturally gluten-free product, many companies process theirs on the same equipment they use for wheat. If you are highly sensitive to gluten or have celiac you want to make sure that you buy gluten-free Masa Harina.

Quinoa Corn Tortillas

Instructions:

1. In a bowl, combine Masa Harina, quinoa, salt, 1¾ cup warm water and lime zest. Mix well and knead with your hands until a Play-Dough–like texture is achieved. Add water as needed 2 tablespoons at a time. If you get cracks in the dough when you flatten it, you need to add more water. Refrigerate dough for 30 minutes. (This step makes the dough easier to work with but is optional.)

2. Shape dough into golf ball-sized balls and cover with a damp towel while you are working.

3. Heat a griddle, cast iron skillet, or other large skillet to medium.

4. Flatten tortillas using a tortilla press, heavy pot, or rolling pin.

5. Cook for 1 to 2 minutes per side, or until the surface appears dry. Place on a plate and cover with a clean, damp dish cloth and foil to keep warm. Store leftovers in a Ziploc bag and refrigerate. Reheat prior to serving. (Tortillas will be the most pliable when fresh.)

6. If you don't want to use all of the dough at once, it can be refrigerated for up to 5 days. Simply add a bit of additional water (¼ cup) to the mixture and cover.

2¼ cups gluten-free Masa Harina
¾ cup cooked quinoa
1¾ – 2¼ cups warm water
1 teaspoon sea salt
1 lime's zest (optional)

{ Servings 12, Calories 87, Fat .9g, Carbohydrates 17.9g, Protein 2.7g, Cholesterol 0mg, Sodium 156mg, Fiber 1.7g, Sugar 0g }

Salads

This salad is so pretty it's sure to liven up any table!

Roasted Acorn Squash, Quinoa & Pomegranate Salad

Instructions:

Dressing

If using chia seeds, combine with water and stir well. Set aside for 10 minutes until a gel forms. In a small bowl whisk together mustard, vinegar, lemon juice, maple syrup, cayenne pepper, and sea salt. Slowly whisk in olive oil or chia gel until well combined.

Salad

Preheat oven to 400 degrees. Line a rimmed baking sheet with parchment paper. Toss squash with olive oil and cook for 15 minutes. Drizzle with maple syrup and cook for 10 minutes more. Cool.

In a medium bowl combine squash, quinoa, and pomegranate seeds. Arrange greens on plates and top with squash mixture. Drizzle with desired amount of dressing and top with almonds. Serve with additional dressing as desired.

Dressing

1 tablespoon Dijon mustard
2 tablespoons apple
   cider vinegar
2 tablespoons lemon juice
¼ cup maple syrup
⅛-¼ teaspoon cayenne
   pepper
½ teaspoon sea salt
½ cup olive oil or 1 tablespoon
   chia seeds
   + ½ cup water

Salad

1 acorn squash, peeled, seeded
   and cut into ½-inch slices
1 tablespoon olive oil
¼ cup maple syrup
1 cup cooked quinoa
½ cup fresh pomegranate seeds
4 cups mixed greens
¼ cup slivered almonds, toasted

Salad: Servings 6, Calories 151, Fat 4.9g, Carbohydrates 25.7g, Protein 3.2g, Cholesterol 0mg, Sodium 15mg, Fiber 2.5g, Sugars 9.7g

Dressing, with Chia Seeds: Servings 8 (approx. 2 tablespoons), Calories 46, Fat 1.4g, Carbohydrates 8.6g, Protein .8, Cholesterol 0mg, Sodium 140mg, Fiber 1.3g, Sugars 6.0g

Dressing, with oil: Servings 8, Calories 137, Fat 12.7g, Carbohydrates 7.1g, Protein .1g, Cholesterol 0mg, Sodium 140mg, Fiber 0g, Sugars 6.0g

This classic combination is made healthier with the addition of quinoa.

Artichoke, Arugula & Quinoa Salad

Instructions:

In a medium bowl combine quinoa, arugula, artichoke hearts, cherries, green onions, and walnuts. Toss with vinaigrette and serve.

2 cups cooked quinoa

4 cups fresh arugula, chopped

14 ounces artichoke hearts, drained and rinsed

¾ cup dried cherries (or cranberries)

4 green onions, chopped

½ cup walnuts, toasted and chopped

⅓ cup balsamic vinaigrette (see p. 269)

Not including dressing: Servings 4, Calories 259, Fat 11.2g, Carbohydrates 33.1g, Protein 11.6g, Cholesterol 0mg, Sodium 103mg, Fiber 9.8g, Sugars 2.6g

This salad is one of my favorite ways to liven things up in the winter! Of course, it is delicious year around.

Avocado, Mango & Pineapple Quinoa Salad

Instructions:

1. If using chia gel in place of oil, combine 3/4 teaspoon chia seeds with 2 tablespoons of water. Mix well and set aside.

2. In a small saucepan, bring champagne or vinegar to a simmer. Add red onion and salt and remove from heat. Allow to cool completely. Drain onions, reserving liquid in a small bowl. Add olive oil or chia gel and basil and whisk together.

3. In a large bowl combine reserved onions, spinach, quinoa, roasted red pepper, mango, pineapple, and avocado.* Toss with dressing and top with nuts if desired.

½ cup chopped red onion

⅓ cup champagne or white or red vinegar

¾ teaspoon sea salt

1 tablespoon basil, chopped

2 tablespoons extra virgin olive oil

2 cups spinach or baby arugula

1 cup cooked quinoa

1 roasted red pepper, diced

1 mango, peeled and diced

1 cup diced and peeled pineapple

1 avocado, peeled and diced

*Note: if you are preparing ahead, wait until you are ready to serve to add the avocado to prevent it from getting discolored.

With Chia Gel: Servings 4, Calories 201, Fat 8.8g, Carbohydrates 30.1g, Protein 4.3g, Cholesterol 0mg, Sodium 413mg, Fiber 6.9g, Sugars 13.3g

With Oil: Servings 4, Calories 257, Fat 12.5g, Carbohydrates 29.7g, Protein 4.1g, Cholesterol 0mg, Sodium 413mg, Fiber 6.6g, Sugars 13.3g

Don't let the long ingredients list of this salad scare you—it comes together quickly. The process goes something like this: make the marinade, whisk the dressing, assemble the salad, grill the chicken, plate the salad, and add the chicken and avocado. Start to finish is less than 30 minutes.

Chicken, Pomegranate & Cashew Quinoa Salad

Instructions:

1. In a small bowl combine lemon juice, sea salt, paprika, and pepper. Whisk until combined. Place tempeh or chicken in a shallow dish and pour the mixture over. Set aside for 15 minutes. In a grill pan or indoor grill, cook until golden brown and cooked through. Allow to cool slightly and cut into thin strips.

2. Meanwhile, make dressing by combining all ingredients in a small bowl and whisking together.

3. In a large bowl combine greens, quinoa, red onion, pomegranate and cashews. Toss until combined. Divide mixture between four plates and top with tempeh or chicken and avocado. Drizzle with dressing and serve.

{ With Tempeh: Servings 4, Calories 421, Fat 23.4g, Carbohydrates 40g, Protein 19.7g, Cholesterol 1mg, Sodium 494mg, Fiber 6.3g, Sugars 14.7g

With Chicken: Servings 4, Calories 391, Fat 17.9, Carbohydrates 33.3g, Protein 27.1g, Cholesterol 56mg, Sodium 532mg, Fiber 6.3g, Sugars 14.7g }

Chicken

10 ounces of tempeh or chicken
2 tablespoons lemon juice
½ teaspoon smoked paprika
½ teaspoon sea salt
⅛ teaspoon black pepper

Dressing

¼ cup plain nonfat Greek
    or soy yogurt
3 tablespoons lemon juice
1–2 cloves garlic, minced
1 tablespoon olive oil
1 teaspoon maple syrup
2 teaspoons white balsamic
    vinegar or white vinegar
½ teaspoon sea salt
¼ teaspoon ground
    black pepper.

Salad

3 cups fresh salad greens
1 cup cooked quinoa
½ red onion, sliced thin
½ cup pomegranate arils
¼ cup cashews
1 avocado, pitted and diced

This pretty salad makes a great addition to a brunch buffet.

Citrus Quinoa Salad

Instructions:

Dressing

If using chia gel, combine chia seeds and water and set aside for 10 minutes. In a small bowl combine orange juice, vinegar, Dijon mustard, maple syrup, and sea salt. Whisk in olive oil or chia gel.

Salad

In a medium bowl combine quinoa, spinach, grapefruit, orange, pomegranate, and red onion. Toss with desired amount of dressing and top with pistachios. (You may not need all of the dressing—especially if your citrus is juicy!)

2 cups cooked quinoa

1 cup baby spinach, chopped

1 pink grapefruit, peeled and sectioned

1 orange, peeled and sectioned

½ cup pomegranate seeds

½ cup finely chopped red onion

3 tablespoons pistachios, chopped

Dressing

2 tablespoons extra virgin olive oil or 1 teaspoon chia seeds + 2 tablespoons water

2 tablespoons fresh orange juice

1 tablespoon champagne or white balsamic vinegar

1 teaspoon Dijon mustard

1 teaspoon maple syrup

½ teaspoon sea salt

{
Servings 4, Calories 174, Fat 4.4g, Carbohydrates 29.1g, Protein 6g, Cholesterol 0mg, Sodium 8mg, Fiber 4.5g, Sugars 7.5g

Dressing, with Chia Seeds: Servings 4, Calories 15, Fat .5g, Carbohydrates 2.5g, Protein .3g, Cholesterol 0mg, Sodium 249mg, Fiber 0g, Sugars 1.7g

Dressing, with Oil: Serves 4, Calories 67, Fat 7.1g, Carbohydrates 2g, Protein .1g, Cholesterol 0mg, Sodium 249mg, Fiber 0g, Sugars 1.7g
}

This recipe was inspired by a kale recipe in Southern Living. *It is pretty enough for your holiday table, but healthy enough to eat every day!*

Roasted Garlic Kale & Quinoa Salad with Cranberries

Instructions:

1. Preheat oven to 375 degrees. Line a rimmed baking pan with parchment paper. Place cranberries and garlic on pan and drizzle with 1 tablespoon of olive oil. Salt and pepper. Roast for 20 to 25 minutes, until cranberries are wrinkled. Cool slightly. Peel and chop garlic.

2. Combine chia seeds and water and set aside for 10 minutes. (Skip this step if you are using olive oil for the dressing.) In a medium jar combine chia gel or olive oil, garlic, lemon juice, maple syrup, mustard, salt, and pepper. Shake well. Pour dressing over kale and massage. Allow kale to sit for 10 minutes.

3. Add quinoa, fennel, walnuts, red pepper, onion, cranberries, and chopped garlic. Toss. Taste. If your cranberries are extremely tart, drizzle with another teaspoon or two of maple syrup and toss again. (You don't want the salad to be sweet; this is just to cut the tartness.)

2 cups fresh cranberries
12 cloves garlic, unpeeled (more or less to taste)
1 tablespoon olive oil
½ tablespoon chia seeds + ¼ cup water or ¼ cup olive oil
¼ cup lemon juice
1 tablespoon Dijon mustard
2 teaspoons maple syrup
4 cups chopped kale
2 cups cooked quinoa
1 small fennel bulb, shaved
1 cup chopped walnuts
½ cup diced red pepper
½ cup thinly sliced red onion

Servings 6, Calories 294, Fat 16.7g, Carbohydrates 31g, Protein 10.6g, Cholesterol 0mg, Sodium 73mg, Fiber 7.2g, Sugars 3.9g

This salad is all about the texture. I just love it's crunchy—nutty—seedy goodness! Not only does it work great as a salad, but it is also fantastic in a wrap. Since it holds well dressed for a couple of days, it's a great make-ahead lunch.

Crunchy Quinoa Salad

Instructions:

1. In a blender combine vinegars, lemon juice, tahini, olive oil, salt, and pepper. Process until smooth.

2. In a large bowl combine quinoa, sprouts, carrot, scallions, sunflower seeds, and almonds. Toss with dressing and season to taste with salt and pepper.

Dressing

1 tablespoon balsamic vinegar
1 tablespoon red wine vinegar
1 tablespoon lemon juice
1 tablespoon tahini
2 tablespoons olive oil
1 teaspoon garlic, minced
1 teaspoon salt
1/4 teaspoon fresh ground black pepper

Salad

3/4 cup cooked Quinoa
3/4 cup lentil or quinoa sprouts (or sprouts of choice)
1 cup grated carrot
2 scallions, sliced thin
1/3 cup sunflower seeds
1/3 cup roasted almonds, chopped

Servings 4, Calories 261, Fat 18.7g, Carbohydrates 17.7g, Protein 8.2g, Cholesterol 0mg, Sodium 719mg, Fiber 3.7g, Sugars 2.3g

This is one of my favorite quinoa salads, and I find myself craving it year-round. It is easy enough for a weeknight meal but is also a beautiful salad for company.

Fall Quinoa Salad with Cranberries, Apple & Walnuts

Instructions:

1. If using chia gel in place of olive oil, combine ¼ cup water with chia seeds. Stir to combine and set aside for 10 minutes.

2. In a blender combine shallot, vinegar, lemon juice, maple syrup, Dijon mustard, salt, and pepper. Process until blended. Add chia gel or olive oil and process until well combined.

3. In a large bowl combine lettuce, arugula, quinoa, dried cranberries, apple, blue cheese, and walnuts. Toss with dressing and serve immediately.

Dressing

¼ cup water + ½ tablespoon chia seeds (or ¼ cup extra virgin olive oil)
1 shallot, minced
2 tablespoons white balsamic vinegar
1 tablespoon lemon juice
1 tablespoon maple syrup
1 teaspoon Dijon mustard
½ teaspoon sea salt
¼ teaspoon fresh ground pepper

Salad

3 cups torn lettuce leaves
3 cups baby arugula
1 cup cooked quinoa
½ cup dried cranberries
1 Granny Smith apple, cored and sliced thin
¼ cup crumbled blue cheese or nondairy blue cheese (optional)
¼ cup walnuts, chopped

Salad: Serves 4, Calories 172, Fat 9g, Carbohydrates 19.8g, Protein 5.9g, Cholesterol 10mg, Sodium 152mg, Fiber 4.7g, Sugars 6.3g

Dressing with Chia Seeds: Serves 4, Calories 26, Fat .7g, Carbohydrates 4.7g, Protein .5g, Cholesterol 0mg, Sodium 249mg, Fiber .7g, Sugars 3.1g

Dressing with Oil: Serves 4, Calories 125, Fat 12.7g, Carbohydrates 3.9g, Protein .1g, Cholesterol 0mg, Sodium 259mg, Fiber 0g, Sugars 3.1g

I love grilled potatoes here, but roasted potatoes work great, too! To roast, bake on a parchment-lined cookie sheet at 375 for 25 to 30 minutes or until tender.

Grilled Sweet Potato & Quinoa Salad

Instructions:

1. If using chia seeds, combine them with water. Stir well and set aside for 10 minutes.

2. Preheat an indoor or outdoor grill to medium high heat.

3. Peel potatoes and cut lengthwise into ¼-inch slices. Combine with 1 tablespoon of olive oil and salt and pepper to taste.

4. Grill over indirect heat (on a grill) or place directly on an indoor grill. Cook for about 15 minutes per side or until tender. Chop to desired size.

5. To make dressing, combine chia gel or oil with lime juice, jalapeño, garlic, and sweet chili sauce. Whisk until combined.

6. Place sweet potatoes, quinoa, corn, scallions, and cilantro in a large bowl. Add dressing and toss until combined.

Salad

2 medium sweet potatoes
1 tablespoon olive oil
1 cup cooked quinoa
1 cup frozen corn, thawed
4 scallions, sliced thin
½ cup chopped cilantro

Dressing

½ cup water + 1 tablespoon chia seeds or ½ cup extra virgin olive oil
⅓ cup lime juice
1 jalapeño, chopped fine
3 cloves garlic, minced
2 tablespoons Thai sweet chili sauce (most are gluten-free but do check the label.)

Servings 4, Calories 248, Fat 6.2g, Carbohydrates 45.6g, Protein 5.6g, Cholesterol 0mg, Sodium 70mg, Fiber 7g, Sugars 5.5g,

This salad is light and refreshing! I use homemade dressing, but if you are short on time, bottled will do. Just make sure to read the label to ensure that it is gluten-free!

Mediterranean Quinoa Salad

Instructions:

1. Bring a pot of water to a boil. Add asparagus and cook for 1 minute. Drain and place in an ice water bath for 5 minutes. Drain and chop into 1-inch pieces.

2. In a large bowl combine quinoa, asparagus, red peppers, grape tomatoes, artichoke hearts, and basil. Toss with balsamic vinegar dressing and serve chilled or at room temperature.

2 cups cooked quinoa

8 ounces fresh asparagus, trimmed

1 red pepper, diced

1 cup grape tomatoes, halved

1 cup drained and chopped water packed artichoke hearts

½ cup fresh basil, chopped

½ cup balsamic vinegar dressing (see p. 269)

Servings 4 (as a side dish), Calories 142, Fat 1.9g, Carbohydrates 25.3g, Protein 6.3g, Cholesterol 0mg, Sodium 6mg, Fiber 5.2g, Sugars 3.3g

Nutritional information does not include dressing.

I originally made this salad for New Year's Day, but now it is one that I enjoy all the time! If you don't have black-eyed peas on hand, try making it with black beans.

Quinoa & Black-Eyed Pea Salad

Instructions:

1. If using chia gel in place of oil, combine 3 tablespoons water with 1 teaspoon chia seeds. Mix well and set aside for 10 to 15 minutes.

2. In a large bowl combine quinoa, black-eyed peas, roasted red pepper, tomato, onion, corn, and cilantro.

3. In a small bowl combine lime juice, garlic, cumin, chipotle chili powder, cilantro, olive oil (or chia gel), and maple syrup. Toss with dressing and season to taste with salt and pepper.

1 cup cooked quinoa
1½ cups cooked black-eyed peas, drained and rinsed (about 1 can)
1 roasted red pepper, diced
1 cup seeded and diced tomato
½ medium red onion, diced
1½ cups frozen corn, thawed
2 tablespoons fresh cilantro, chopped

Dressing
3 tablespoons fresh lime juice
1 teaspoon minced garlic
1 teaspoon ground cumin
⅛ teaspoon chipotle chili powder
1 tablespoon fresh cilantro, finely chopped
3 tablespoons olive oil or chia gel
1 tablespoon maple syrup
Salt and pepper to taste

With Chia Gel: Servings 4, Calories 205, Fat 2.8g, Carbohydrates 39.9g, Protein 9.0g, Cholesterol 0mg, Sodium 74mg, Fiber 6.7g, Sugars 6.4g

With Olive Oil: Servings 4, Calories 290, Fat 12.9g, Carbohydrates 39.4g, Protein 8.7g, Cholesterol 0mg, Sodium 74mg, Fiber 6.3g, Sugars 6.4g

I absolutely love the pickled onions in this salad, but if you are short on time, feel free to use raw chopped onions.

Quinoa Salad with Garbanzo Beans, Sun Dried Tomatoes & Pickled Onions

Instructions:

1. Place red wine vinegar and water in a small saucepan. Bring to a boil and add onions. Remove from heat and add salt and pepper. Allow to sit for 5 minutes or more and drain. (The onions may be made ahead of time and stored in their liquid in the refrigerator.)

2. Combine all ingredients in a bowl. Toss with dressing and serve at room temperature or chilled.

½ cup red wine vinegar
¼ cup water
½ cup red onion, chopped
1 cup cooked quinoa
1 cup cooked garbanzo beans, drained
½ cup sun dried tomatoes, rehydrated and chopped
½ cup fresh basil, chopped
Balsamic vinegar dressing, to taste (see p. 269)

Nutritional information excluding dressing: Servings 4, Calories 151, Fat 3.3g, Carbohydrates 24.5g, Protein 5.8g, Cholesterol 0mg, Sodium 150mg, Fiber 2g, Sugars 3.7g,

This easy-to-make salad is taken up a notch by roasting the garlic and tomatoes. If you are short on time, feel free to use purchased balsamic vinegar dressing.

Roasted Tomato, Corn & Quinoa Salad

Instructions:

1. Preheat oven to 420 degrees. Toss tomatoes, garlic, and olive oil in a medium bowl. Place on a parchment-lined rimmed baking sheet and bake for 13 to 15 minutes.

2. Meanwhile, in a medium bowl combine quinoa, corn, and red onion.

3. When tomatoes are done add to the quinoa mixture, being sure to get all of the garlic from the pan. Toss with dressing and serve.

1 cup grape or cherry tomatoes
4 cloves garlic, minced
½ Tablespoon olive oil
2 cups cooked quinoa
1 cup frozen organic corn, thawed
1 red onion, sliced thin
Balsamic vinegar
    dressing (see p. 269)

dressing (see p. 269)

Nutritional information not including dressing: Servings 4, Calories 177, Fat 4g, Carbohydrates 31.9g, Protein 5.6g, Cholesterol 0mg, Sodium 9mg, Fiber 3.7g, Sugars 6.2g.

Though I usually use white quinoa in my cooking, this is one case where the firmer texture of red or black quinoa really pays off!

Southwestern Quinoa & Pasta Salad

Instructions:

1. If using chia gel in place of olive oil, combined 3 tablespoons of water and 1 teaspoon of chia seeds. Mix well and set aside.*

2. Cook quinoa pasta according to package directions, being careful not to over or under cook. Drain and rinse. Toss with 1/2 tablespoon of olive oil.

3. In a small bowl combine lime juice, olive oil or chia gel, chipotle pepper, garlic, cilantro, salt, and pepper.

4. Combined cooked pasta with quinoa, beans, tomato, corn, red pepper, jalapeño, and red pepper. Toss with dressing, reserving a little if desired. When ready to serve add in avocado and additional dressing if desired.

*Note: if you are planning on making this salad ahead of time, the pasta will keep best with the addition of oil. If you don't want to use the full 3 tablespoons for the dressing, simply toss the pasta with a little olive oil just after cooking.

With Oil: Servings 8, Calories 328, Fat 11.7g, Carbohydrates 47.5g, Protein 11.8g, Cholesterol 0mg, Sodium 130mg, Fiber 9.9g, Sugars 3.6g

With Chia Seeds (but still tossing pasta with oil): Servings 8, Calories 286, Fat 6.6g, Carbohydrates 47.5, Protein 11.9, Cholesterol 0mg, Sodium 130mg, Fiber 10.1g, Sugars 3.6g

8 ounces uncooked fusilli or elbow quinoa pasta
½ tablespoon of olive oil (for pasta)
1 cup cooked red or rainbow quinoa
1 ½ cup black beans, drained and rinsed (about one can)
1 large tomato, diced
1 cup frozen corn, thawed
1 red pepper, diced
1 jalapeño pepper, seeded and diced
1 medium red onion, diced
1 avocado, pitted and iced

Dressing
¼ cup lime juice
3 tablespoons extra virgin olive oil or 3 tablespoons water + 1 teaspoon chia seeds
1–2 chipotle pepper in adobo sauce, minced
3 cloves garlic, minced
½ cup fresh cilantro, chopped
½ teaspoon sea salt
½ teaspoon fresh ground black pepper

Tortilla Quinoa Salad with Cilantro Lime Dressing

Instructions

1. Preheat oven to 350 degrees. Cut tortillas in half and then into ¼-inch strips. Place on a baking sheet and spray with olive oil spray. Salt and pepper to taste. Bake about 10 minutes, turning half way through.

2. Meanwhile, if using chia gel in place of the oil in the dressing combine chia seeds and water. Stir well and set aside.

3. In a large bowl combine lettuce, quinoa, black beans, tomatoes, red onion, and avocado.

4. Make dressing by combining all ingredients in a food processor or blender and processing until smooth.

5. Toss salad with desired amount of dressing and top with tortilla strips.

6 corn tortillas

Olive oil spray

3 cups chopped romaine lettuce

2 cups cooked quinoa

1 ½ cups cooked black beans, drained and rinsed (about 1 can)

1 cup cherry or grape tomatoes, quartered

1 medium red onion, chopped

1 avocado, pitted, peeled and diced

Cilantro Lime Dressing

¼ cup fresh lime juice

2 tablespoons maple syrup (or other liquid sweetener)

1 tablespoon balsamic vinegar

1 jalapeño seeded and diced

2 cloves garlic, minced

½ cup fresh cilantro leaves, chopped

½ cup water + 1 tablespoon chia seeds or ½ cup olive oil

1 teaspoon sea salt

Servings 6, Calories 285, Fat 7.7g, Carbohydrates 46.9g, Protein 10.1g, Cholesterol 0 mg, Sodium 410mg, Fiber 11.3g, Sugars 9.4g

Tabbouleh is a Middle Eastern dish that is typically made with bulgur. A less traditional but still common alternative is to make it with couscous. I, of course, shun both of these options and make mine with quinoa. To mix things up a little more, I've added spinach, roasted red pepper, and a splash of tamari. The result is a bright, fresh, and flavorful dish that also happens to be quite versatile.

Spinach Quinoa Tabbouleh

Instructions:

1. If using chia gel in place of oil, combine chia seeds and water and stir well. Set aside for 10 minutes, or until a gel forms.

2. Combine spinach, mint, and parsley in a food processor and pulse until chopped. Add in garlic, lemon juice, soy sauce or tamari, and olive oil or chia gel and pulse a few more times until well combined.

3. In a large bowl combine quinoa, grape tomatoes, cucumber, and roasted red pepper. Top with spinach mixture and stir until combined.

5 cups spinach

¼ cup fresh mint

¼ cup fresh parsley (or cilantro)

4 cloves garlic, minced

¼ cup lemon juice

2 tablespoons soy sauce or gluten-free tamari

¼ cup extra virgin olive oil or ½ tablespoon chia seeds + ¼ cup water

2 cups cooked quinoa

2 cups grape tomatoes, halved

½ cucumber, peeled and chopped

1 roasted red pepper, chopped

With Chia Gel: Servings 4, Calories 255, Fat 14.7g, Carbohydrates 27.5g, Protein 7g, Cholesterol 0mg, Sodium 534mg, Fiber 4.7g, Sugars 4.1g

With Olive Oil: Servings 4, Calories 156, Fat 2.7g, Carbohydrates 28.3g, Protein 7.3g, Cholesterol 0mg, Sodium 534mg, Fiber 5.3g, Sugars 4.1g

This protein-packed salad makes a fantastic lunch! For a change of pace, try incorporating your leftovers into a wrap.

Mexican Roasted Chickpea & Quinoa Salad

Instructions:

1. Preheat oven to 400 degrees. Line a rimmed baking sheet with parchment paper. In bowl combine chickpeas, corn, red pepper, taco seasoning, lime juice, and soy sauce. Toss until well combined. Add chickpeas to baking sheet and roast for 35 to 45 minutes, stirring often to prevent the vegetables from burning.

2. Combine lime juice and agave nectar in a small bowl. In a large bowl combine quinoa, tomatoes, jalapeño, cilantro, and chickpea mixture. Toss with lime juice and serve warm or at room temperature.

1½ cups cooked chickpeas, drained and rinsed (about 1 can)

1½ cups frozen corn, thawed

1 red pepper, seeded and diced

2 tablespoons taco seasoning

2 tablespoons lime juice

2 tablespoons soy sauce

1½ cups cooked quinoa

1 large tomato, seeded and diced

1 jalapeño, seeded and diced

2 tablespoons cilantro, chopped fine

2 tablespoons lime juice

1 teaspoon agave nectar or maple syrup

Servings 4, Calories 243, Fat 2.8g, Carbohydrates 46.9g, Protein 10.4g, Cholesterol 0mg, Sodium 630mg, Fiber 4.3g, Sugars 10.2g

If you are starting with dried black beans, try putting in a teaspoon of smoked paprika per cup of dried beans! Similarly, if you don't already have quinoa cooked and are cooking it specifically for this recipe (or for this and any other Mexican-style quinoa), add in a teaspoon of smoked paprika per cup of uncooked quinoa.

Smoky Black Bean & Poblano Pepper Quinoa Salad

Instructions:

In a medium bowl combine black beans, quinoa, red pepper, red onion, tomato, poblano pepper, and cilantro. Toss with desired amount of dressing (I used about half) and serve at room temperature or chilled. Drizzle with additional dressing and top with avocado and/or sour cream if desired.

Dressing

If you are using chia seeds for the dressing, combine chia seeds and 1/3 cup water and set aside for 10 to 15 minutes, until a gel forms.

In a small bowl or jar combine lime juice, Dijon mustard, smoked paprika, chipotle chili powder, and sea salt. Stir or shake to combine. Add olive oil or chia gel and whisk or shake until well combined.

1½ cups cooked black beans, drained and rinsed
1½ cups cooked quinoa
2 roasted red bell peppers, diced
1 cup diced red onion
1 tomato, seeded and diced
1 poblano pepper, seeded and diced
⅓ cup chopped fresh cilantro

For Topping
1 avocado, pitted and diced
4 tablespoons (vegan) sour cream or Greek yogurt

Dressing
⅓ cup fresh lime juice
2 teaspoons Dijon mustard
1 teaspoon smoked paprika
¼ teaspoon chipotle chili powder
½ teaspoon sea salt
⅓ cup water + 2 teaspoons chia seeds or ⅓ cup olive oil

Servings 4, Calories 303, Fat 9.9g, Carbohydrates 42g, Protein 2.9g, Cholesterol 0mg, Sodium 376mg, Fiber 14.6g, Sugars 7.5g

I've always loved ordering taco salads in restaurants, but unfortunately most are far from healthy. Here is a healthier version and you won't miss a thing!

Quinoa Taco Salad Bowls

Instructions:

1. For serving: gluten-free tortilla chips OR gluten-free tortilla bowl (see below), sour cream/Greek yogurt.

2. Spray a medium skillet well with olive oil spray. Add chopped onion and cook for 10 to 12 minutes, until tender. Add garlic, taco seasoning, chipotle chili, and quinoa. Cook for 2 minutes, stirring frequently. Add vegetable broth and bring to a simmer. Reduce to low and cook for 30 to 35 minutes.

3. Stir in lime juice, pinto beans, corn, and cilantro. Cover and let sit off the heat for 5 minutes. Fluff.

4. Fill bowls (either regular or tortilla bowls) with romaine lettuce. Top with quinoa mixture, cheese, avocado and salsa. Serve with tortilla chips and sour cream or Greek yogurt.

5. To make the salad bowls, place tortillas over a tortilla baker or over a can that has been covered with aluminum foil and coated in cooking spray. Bake for 10 minutes or until crispy.

Olive oil spray
1 medium onion, chopped
3 cloves garlic, minced
2 teaspoons taco seasoning
½–1 chipotle chili pepper in adobo sauce, chopped fine
½ cup quinoa, rinsed
1 cup vegetable broth
1 lime, juiced
2 cups cooked pinto beans (about 1 can)
1½ cups frozen corn, thawed
¼ cup chopped cilantro
6 cups romaine lettuce
½ cup grated cheddar or Daiya
1 avocado, sliced
1 cup salsa

Servings 6, Calories 267 (not including chips/bowl/sour cream), Fat 10.1g, Carbohydrates 36.1g, Protein 11.5g, Cholesterol 10mg, Sodium 657mg, Fiber 8.9g, Sugars 4.9g

This protein-packed salad makes a fantastic lunch!

Edamame Quinoa Salad

Instructions:

1. If using chia gel in place of oil, combine chia seeds and water and mix well. Set aside until a gel forms.

2. In a large bowl combine edamame, cabbage, quinoa, diced pepper, pineapple, raisins, and almonds.

3. In a small bowl combine red wine vinegar, olive oil or chia gel, coconut palm sugar, chili powder, and garlic. Toss with quinoa mixture and serve either chilled or at room temperature.

1½ cups frozen edamame, cooked according to package directions

2 cups red cabbage, shredded

2 cups cooked quinoa

1 red pepper, seeded and diced small

¾ cup diced pineapple

¼ cup raisins

2 teaspoons almonds, chopped

2 tablespoons red wine vinegar

2 tablespoons olive oil or

    2 tablespoons water

    + ¾ teaspoon chia seeds

1 teaspoon coconut palm sugar

1 teaspoon chili powder

3 cloves garlic, minced

With Chia Gel: Servings 4, Calories 246, Fat 2.46g, Carbohydrates 39.7g, Protein 11.2g, Cholesterol 0mg, Sodium 25mg, Fiber 6.5g, Sugars 12.6g

With Oil: Servings 4, Calories 302, Fat 12.2g, Carbohydrates 39.4g, Protein 11g, Cholesterol 0mg, Sodium 25mg, Fiber 6.2g, Sugars 12.6g

Wraps, Burgers, Tacos & Sandwiches

One thing I love about veggie burgers is that they are easy to make ahead and freeze well. I often make a double batch and then freeze the uncooked patties so I have something on hand for those times when the boys are hungry and need something quick.

Black Bean & Quinoa Burgers

Instructions:

1. Heat a large skillet over medium heat and spray well with olive oil spray. Add onion and sun dried tomatoes and cook for 8 to 10 minutes. Add garlic and cook for an additional 30 seconds.

2. Meanwhile, if using flax eggs combine 2 tablespoons of ground flax seeds with 6 tablespoons of warm water. Stir well and set aside.

3. Place half of the onion mixture, half of the quinoa, half of the black beans in a food processor and blend for 2 minutes, until smooth. Transfer to a bowl and add remaining onion mixture, quinoa, beans, gluten-free flour, barbecue sauce, liquid smoke, sea salt, and pepper. Stir until well combined. Add eggs or flax eggs and mix well. Using your hands, form into 6 patties. If desired, you can refrigerate for at least 30 minutes to help the patties hold together better.

4. Melt coconut oil in a large skillet over medium heat. Make sure your pan is warm before adding your patties. Add the patties and cook for about 8 minutes per side, flipping once. Your patties will be ready to flip when the edges turn brown.

1 large onion, diced

½ cup sun dried tomatoes, rehydrated

1 teaspoon minced garlic

1 ½ cups cooked quinoa

1 ½ cups black beans, drained and rinsed (about 1 can)

¼ cup all purpose gluten-free quinoa flour blend (see p. 30)

2 tablespoons gluten-free barbecue sauce

2 teaspoons liquid smoke (optional)

1 teaspoon sea salt

½ teaspoon fresh ground black pepper

2 eggs or flax eggs (2 tablespoons ground flax seeds + 6 tablespoons warm water)

2 tablespoons coconut oil, for cooking

Servings 6, Calories 222, Fat 8.2g, Carbohydrates 28.8g, Protein 9.4g, Cholesterol 55mg, Sodium 496mg, Fiber 6.4g, Sugars 3.5g

Our family loves tacos and every now and then I like to put a new twist on our old favorite. Give this one a try and you will see why mixing it up every now and then can be fun!

Curried Quinoa Tacos with Garlic Lime Cream Sauce

Instructions:

1. If you are using crunchy taco shells, heat oven according to package directions.

2. Spray a large skillet well with olive oil and add onion. Cook for 8 to 12 minutes, until tender. Add quinoa, tempeh (or ground meat), cilantro, curry powder, turmeric, and mango chutney. Stir until well combined and cook for 5 to 7 minutes. Remove from heat and stir in lime juice.

3. Meanwhile, if you are using corn tortillas, heat a small skillet to medium. Heat tortillas a few minutes per side to make pliable. Wrap in foil to keep warm. Alternatively, bake taco shells according to package directions.

4. Make cream sauce by mixing yogurt, lime zest, lime juice, and garlic in a small bowl

5. Top heated tortillas or taco shells with tempeh (or ground meat)/quinoa mixture, red pepper, and shredded cabbage. Drizzle with yogurt mixture and top with cashews.

1 sweet onion

1 cup cooked quinoa

8 ounces tempeh, shredded or browned ground meat of choice

½ cup fresh cilantro, chopped

2 teaspoons hot curry powder

1 teaspoon turmeric

¾ cup hot mango chutney (make sure it is gluten-free)

1 tablespoon fresh lime juice

8 corn tortillas or crunchy taco shells

½ red bell pepper, chopped

2 cups shredded cabbage

¼ cup chopped cashews

Garlic Lime Cream Sauce

½ cup Greek yogurt, nonfat dairy or nondairy

1 teaspoon lime zest

2 tablespoons lime juice

2 cloves garlic, minced

Servings 8, Calories 210, Fat 6g, Carbohydrates 29.2g, Protein 11.6g, Cholesterol 2mg, Sodium 75mg, Fiber 5.6g, Sugars 6.0g

This refreshing wrap is the perfect way to fuel your day! Try adding in ½ cup cooked garbanzo beans for a variation.

Grilled Vegetable Quinoa Wraps with Spicy Sauce

Instructions:

1. Heat an indoor grill to medium high heat. In a medium bowl toss red onion, red pepper, and zucchini with olive oil. Grill for 6 to 8 minutes per side, or until tender and lightly browned.

2. Heat tortillas in a dry skillet until they are pliable. Spread 1 tablespoon of spicy sauce on each tortilla. Top with spinach, sprouts, ¼ cup quinoa and a quarter of the vegetables. Fold the bottom part of the tortilla over the vegetables and roll up tightly. Cut in half on the diagonal and serve.

3. Combine ingredients in a small bowl and whisk together. Store in the refrigerator until ready to serve.

4 gluten-free wraps

1 red onion, sliced thin

1 red pepper, cut into
    ½-inch strips

1 small zucchini, cut into
    1-inch rounds

1 tablespoon extra virgin
    olive oil

1 cup cooked quinoa

1 cup alfalfa sprouts (or sprout
    of choice)

1 cup baby spinach

¼ cup spicy sauce

Spicy Sauce

½ cup Greek yogurt or
    tofu mayo

1 tablespoon Sriracha

2 tablespoons Dijon mustard

2 teaspoons minced garlic

½ teaspoon fresh ground
    black pepper

Servings 4, Calories 241, Fat 8g, Carbohydrates 34.4g, Protein 15.7g, Cholesterol 1mg, Sodium 517mg, Fiber 11g, Sugars 5.2g

Nutritional information uses 100 calorie wrap.

This easy-to-make wrap is packed with flavor!

Guacamole Quinoa Wraps

Instructions:

1. In a large bowl combine quinoa, black beans, red peppers, tomato, and red onion. Sprinkle with taco seasoning and stir until combined.

2. Place the wraps on a flat surface. Spread with 2 tablespoons of guacamole. Add ¼ of the quinoa mixture and top with lettuce. Wrap and serve.

1 ¼ cups cooked quinoa

1 ½ cups black beans, drained and rinsed

⅓ cup roasted red peppers, drained, rinsed and chopped

½ cup grape or cherry tomatoes, quartered

⅓ cup red onion, chopped

1 ½ tablespoons taco seasoning

4 large brown rice tortillas

½ cup guacamole

1 ½ cups chopped lettuce

Servings 4, Calories 307, Fat 6.2g, Carbohydrates 50.1g, Protein 13.6g, Cholesterol 0mg, Sodium 453mg, Fiber 11.7g, Sugars 5.4g

I love serving this for a light luncheon with friends! It's healthy but oh-so-delicious.

Mediterranean Chicken Lettuce Cups

Instructions:

1. Heat a large skillet to medium heat. Spray with olive oil and add tempeh or chicken. Sprinkle with oregano, parsley, salt and pepper. Cook until browned and cooked through. Add in quinoa, onion, artichoke hearts, black olives, capers, and tomatoes. Cook for 4 to 6 more minutes.

2. Spoon mixture into each lettuce leaf and drizzle with a ½ tablespoon of balsamic vinegar dressing.

10 ounces tempeh or chicken, diced

½ teaspoon salt

¼ teaspoon fresh ground black pepper

1 teaspoon fresh oregano or ¼ teaspoon dried

1 tablespoon fresh parsley or 1 teaspoon dried

1 ½ cups cooked quinoa

1 red onion, sliced

½ cup canned artichoke hearts, drained and diced

½ cup pitted black olives, drained and chopped

1 tablespoon capers, drained and chopped

1 plum tomato, seeded and diced

12 bibb or butter lettuce leaves, washed and separated

6 tablespoons balsamic vinegar dressing (see p. 269)

With tempeh: Servings 6, Calories 189, Fat 6.7g, Carbohydrates 22g, Protein 11.5g, Cholesterol 0mg, Sodium 357mg, Fiber 8.2g, Sugars 1.3g

With Chicken: Servings 6, Calories 160, Fat 3.6g, Carbohydrates 15.2g, Protein 16.8g, Cholesterol 36mg, Sodium 383mg, Fiber 4.4g, Sugars 1.3g

According to research in Nutrition & Metabolism, *the resistant starch found in chickpeas could help you burn up to 23% more fat! I love to make these over the weekend so I have something healthy to grab when I'm in a hurry.*

Chickpea Cakes with Cucumber Sauce

Instructions:

1. Make flax eggs by combining flax seeds with warm water and setting aside.

2. Place quinoa flakes in a food processor and process until smooth. Add in chickpeas, quinoa, and chickpea flour and process until mostly pureed but some large chunks remain.

3. In a medium bowl combine flax eggs, tahini, cilantro, scallions, red pepper, chili powder, cayenne pepper, salt, and pepper. Stir in processed quinoa mixture and form into 8 equal patties, about ½ cup each.

4. Heat oil over medium heat. Add patties and cook until brown, about 6 minutes per side. Patties are ready to be flipped when the edges start to brown.

5. Serve with cucumber sauce.

6. To make the sauce, place shredded cucumber in a colander over a bowl.

7. Sprinkle with salt and allow to sit for 20 minutes. Combine cucumber, sour cream, lime juice, cilantro, garlic, and scallions in a medium bowl. Salt and pepper to taste. Refrigerate until ready to use.

Patties: Servings 8, Calories 255, Fat 7.9g, Carbohydrates 34.5g, Protein 11.2g, Cholesterol 0mg, Sodium 130mg, Fiber 7.6g, Sugars 2.2g

Sauce, with Follow Your Heart Sour Cream: Servings 8, Calories 56, Fat 4.8g, Carbohydrates 4.9g, Protein .4g, Cholesterol 0 mg, Sodium 45mg, Fiber 2.2g, Sugars .8g

Sauce, with nonfat Greek Yogurt: Servings 8, Calories 26, Fat .1g, Carbohydrates 3.2g, Protein 3.4g, Cholesterol 2mg, Sodium 32mg, Fiber 0g, Sugars 1.8g

¾ cup quinoa flakes
3 cups chickpeas, drained and rinsed (about 2 cans)
2 cups cooked quinoa
½ cup chickpea flour
2 eggs or flax eggs (2 tablespoons flax seeds + 6 tablespoons warm water)
2 tablespoons tahini
¼ cup cilantro, chopped
3 scallions, sliced thin
¼ cup chopped red pepper
1 teaspoon chili powder
⅛ teaspoon cayenne pepper
½ teaspoon sea salt
½ teaspoon fresh ground black pepper
1 tablespoon coconut oil (more as needed)

Sauce
1 cucumber, peeled, seeded, and shredded
1 cup nondairy sour cream or Greek yogurt
1 tablespoon fresh lime juice
¼ cup fresh cilantro, chopped
2 cloves garlic, minced
2 scallions, sliced thin
Salt and pepper

This is an easy-to-make wrap that can be enjoyed either warm or cold.

Wraps, Burgers, Tacos & Sandwiches

Spicy Mexican Quinoa Wrap

Instructions:

1. In a blender or food processor, combine tofu, salsa, nutritional yeast, chipotle chili, and garlic. Process until smooth.

2. In a large bowl combine quinoa, corn, black beans, and cilantro. Add ¼ cup tofu mixture and toss. Add ¼ of quinoa mixture, avocado, and tomato to each tortilla and drizzle with additional sauce. Roll up and serve with additional sauce on the side.

3. If you would like to enjoy this wrap warm, heat a skillet to medium low heat and add 2 tablespoons of olive oil. Cook until golden brown. Alternatively, heat sandwich in a non, stick griddle or indoor sandwich press until golden brown.

½ cup organic silken tofu

½ cup salsa

2 tablespoons nutritional yeast (optional)

1 chipotle chili (from a can of chipotle chili peppers in adobo sauce)

2 cloves garlic, minced

1 cup cooked quinoa

1 cup organic corn, thawed

1 cup cooked black beans

¼ cup fresh cilantro, chopped

1 avocado, diced

1 tomato, diced

4 large gluten-free wraps

Olive oil, for cooking (optional)

Servings 4, Calories 381, Fat 12.9g, Carbohydrates 61.5g, Protein 18.5g, Cholesterol 0mg, Sodium 674mg, Fiber 20g, Sugars 4.4g

Kids and adults alike can't resist the comfort of Sloppy Joes! To make this recipe a bit more kid friendly, leave off the chipotle chili powder and have the adults add hot sauce to their individual sandwiches!

Barbecued Quinoa Sloppy Joes

Instructions:

1. Place a skillet over medium heat and spray with olive oil. Add onion and pepper and cook for 8 to 10 minutes.

2. Add garlic, salt, pepper, chili powder and chipotle chili powder and cook for 30 more seconds.

3. Stir in cooked quinoa and steamed tempeh or browned ground beef. Cook for 4 to 5 minutes, or until heated through.

4. Add in maple syrup, tomato sauce, barbecue sauce, Worcestershire sauce, tamari, water and hot sauce. Salt and pepper to taste.

5. Simmer for 8 to 10 minutes. Spoon mixture onto buns and top with pickles if desired.

Olive oil spray
1 onion, chopped fine
1 red or green bell pepper, chopped fine
3 cloves garlic, minced
1 teaspoon salt
¼ teaspoon fresh ground black pepper
1 teaspoon chili powder
¼ teaspoon chipotle chili powder
1 cup cooked quinoa
8 ounces steamed tempeh, chopped small or browned ground meat of choice
1 tablespoon maple syrup
8 ounces gluten-free tomato sauce
½ cup gluten-free barbecue sauce
2 tablespoons Worcestershire sauce
2 tablespoons gluten free tamari
2 tablespoons water
¼ teaspoon hot sauce (more or less depending on taste and brand)
6 gluten-free hamburger buns
Pickles, optional

{
With Tempeh: Servings 6, Calories 382, Fat 9.5g, Carbohydrates 62.2g, Protein 14.2g, Cholesterol 0mg, Sodium 1474mg, Fiber 9.2g, Sugars 15.2g

With Ground Beef: Servings 6, Calories 372, Fat 8.1g, Carbohydrates 56.9g, Protein 19g, Cholesterol 34mg, Sodium 1495mg, Fiber 6.2g, Sugars 15.2g
}

This is one of my go-to meals for the boys! It's easily adaptable for different tastes, making it perfect for my picky family.

Veggie & Quinoa Burrito

Instructions:

1. Spray a medium saucepan with organic canola spray. Add onion and jalapeño and cook for 8 to 10 minutes, until tender. Add quinoa and garlic and sauté for one minute. Add vegetable broth and bring to a simmer. Reduce heat to low and cover. Cook for 30 to 35 minutes. Remove from heat and allow to sit covered for 5 more minutes.

2. In a small bowl combine sour cream, cilantro, lime juice, and chipotle chili pepper.

3. Heat a large skillet to medium high heat and spray with canola oil spray. Add corn and zucchini and cook for 2 minutes. Add tomatoes and cook for one additional minute. Remove vegetables from heat and wipe pan carefully with paper towels.

4. Heat tortillas a few minutes per side. Spread with a thin layer of sour cream. Top with ¼ cup cheese, ¼ of the quinoa, and ¼ of the vegetable mixture. Roll up using toothpicks to secure.

5. Return skillet to medium heat and spray with olive oil. Add 2 burritos to pan and cook each side until browned.

1 onion, chopped
1 jalapeño, seeded and minced (optional)
½ cup quinoa, rinsed
4 cloves garlic, minced
⅔ cup gluten-free vegetable broth
⅓ cup vegan or low fat sour cream or Greek yogurt
1 tablespoon chopped fresh cilantro
2 teaspoons lime juice
⅛ tablespoon chipotle chili pepper powder (optional)
1 cup frozen corn, thawed
¾ cup shredded zucchini
¾ cup chopped tomatoes
4 gluten-free tortillas
1 cup Daiya pepper jack or cheddar cheese
For serving: salsa and/or guacamole (optional)

With Daiya: Servings 4, Calories 385, Fat 12.9g, Carbohydrates 57.8, Protein 9.5g, Cholesterol 8mg, Sodium 558mg, Fat 6.6g, Sugars 3.7g

With Cheddar: Servings 4, Calories 409, Fat 16.3g, Carbohydrates 51.1g, Protein 15.5g, Cholesterol 38mg, Sodium 483mg, Fiber 5.6g, Sugars 3.9g

Without Cheese: Servings 4, Calories 295, Fat 7g, Carbohydrates 50.8, Protein 8.5g, Cholesterol 8mg, Sodium 308mg, Fiber 5.6g, Sugars 3.7g

Nutritional information assumes 130-calorie wrap

I'm a big fan of wraps for an easy summer dinner!

Waldorf Salad Wraps

Instructions:

1. Combine chia seeds and water and stir well. Allow to sit for 10 minutes to thicken. (Skip this step if you are using olive oil.)

2. In a small bowl combine chia gel or oil, rice wine vinegar, lemon juice, cayenne pepper, salt, and pepper. Whisk well until combined.

3. In a large bowl combine quinoa, toasted walnuts, apple, celery, grapes, and blue cheese. Toss with dressing. Taste and add salt and pepper to taste.

4. Heat wraps in a large dry skillet for 1 to 2 minutes per side, or until pliable.

5. Put ½ tablespoon of mayonnaise on each wrap and top with greens and quinoa mixture. Fold the ends in and wrap. Cut in half and serve.

Dressing

3 tablespoons water
    + 1 teaspoon chia seeds
    (or 3 tablespoons olive oil)
2 tablespoons rice wine vinegar
1 tablespoon fresh lemon juice
⅛–¼ teaspoon cayenne pepper
½ teaspoon black pepper
½ teaspoon sea salt

Filling

2 cups cooked quinoa
½ cup chopped walnuts, toasted
1 Granny Smith apple, chopped
¾ cup celery, chopped
1½ cups red seedless
    grapes, halved
½ cup crumbled blue cheese,
    regular or nondairy (optional)
3 cups mixed greens
3 tablespoons tofu mayo,
    Veganaise or low fat
    mayonnaise (optional)
6 gluten-free or whole
    wheat wraps

Servings 6, Calories 355, Fat 15.7g, Carbohydrates 51.4g, Protein 13.4g, Cholesterol 8mg, Sodium 729mg, Fiber 12g, Sugars 10.2g

This is one of my husband's all-time favorite quinoa recipes! If you have never tried tempeh, I encourage you to give it a try.

Chipotle Quinoa Tacos

Instructions:

1. Steam tempeh for 10 minutes and set aside to cool.

2. In a blender or food processor combine chipotle peppers, adobo sauce, lime juice, soy sauce, olive oil, taco seasoning, sweetener, and garlic. Add liquid smoke (if using) and water. Process until smooth and transfer to a bowl.

3. Place tempeh in a dry food processor and process until it is the consistency of ground beef. (You can also use a hand grater.) Place tempeh in the bowl with the marinade and stir well. Add quinoa and stir until well combined. Allow to marinade for one hour or overnight.

4. Preheat oven and bake taco shells according to package directions.

5. Meanwhile, heat a skillet over medium heat and spray well with olive oil. (If you want the mixture to get crispy, add a little more oil.) Add tempeh and quinoa mixture and cook for 7 to 9 minutes. (I like to add ½ cup Daiya cheese in the last couple of minutes of cooking.)

6. Line warm shells with tempeh/quinoa mixture and top with desired fixings.

8 ounces tempeh*
1 ½ cups cooked quinoa
2 chipotle chili peppers +
    1 tablespoon adobo sauce
2 limes, juiced
1 tablespoon soy sauce
1 tablespoon olive oil
2 tablespoons taco seasoning
1 tablespoon agave nectar,
    honey or maple syrup
4 cloves garlic, minced
1 teaspoon liquid smoke
    (optional)
⅓ cup water
1 box taco shells (12)
For serving: shredded lettuce,
    corn, chopped red onions,
    chopped tomatoes, salsa,
    cheese, sour cream

*Note: If you don't want to use tempeh, there are several other options to enjoy these tacos. One alternative is to use 3 cups of cooked quinoa. For you meat eaters, simply half the marinade and use it on the meat (ground beef or chopped chicken). Cook the meat through and then add the quinoa once your meat is cooked.

Servings 12, Calories per taco (not including fixings) 145, Fat 6.2g, Carbohydrates 17.6g, Protein 5.4g, Cholesterol 0g, Sodium 130mg, Fiber 2.9g, Sugar 1.1g

There are a couple of secrets to great quinoa patties. The first is starting with a pan that is already heated. Depending on your stove, this can mean allowing your pan to heat for 10 to 15 minutes before you add the oil. Secondly, you want to make sure that a golden crust has formed before you flip the patties. You will be able to see the edges start to turn brown and the patties will look noticeably dryer on top.

Curried Sweet Potato Quinoa Patties with Spicy Yogurt Sauce

Instructions:

1. Make flax eggs by combining 4 tablespoons ground flax seeds with ¾ cup water. Set aside. (Skip this step if you are using eggs).

2. Spray a pan with olive oil and heat to medium. Add onion and cook until tender, about 10 minutes. Add garlic and cook for 30 seconds more. Remove from heat and transfer to a bowl.

3. Combine (flax) egg, cornmeal, hot mango chutney, curry powder, turmeric, cumin, sea salt, and pepper in medium bowl. Whisk until well combined. Add to onion mixture and stir in sweet potatoes, quinoa, and green peas. Form into 12 patties with your hands. Place in the refrigerator for 30 minutes.

4. Heat coconut oil to medium high heat. Cover and cook fritters about 6 minutes per side, flipping once after a brown crust has formed.
Combine all ingredients in a small bowl and whisk together. Refrigerate until ready to serve.

4 eggs or flax eggs
(¼ cup ground flax seeds
+ ¾ cup warm water)
Olive oil spray
1 large onion, diced
1 teaspoon minced garlic
½ cup fine yellow cornmeal
2 tablespoons gluten-free hot mango chutney
1 tablespoon curry powder
1 teaspoon turmeric
½ teaspoon ground cumin
½ teaspoon sea salt
½ teaspoon black pepper
3 cups grated sweet potatoes
2 cups cooked quinoa
½ cup frozen green peas, thawed
2 tablespoons coconut oil (more as needed)

Spicy Yogurt Sauce
½ cup plain nonfat Greek yogurt or soy yogurt
1 tablespoon hot mango chutney
1 teaspoon onion powder
½ teaspoon curry powder
⅛ teaspoon cayenne pepper
½ teaspoon sea salt

Servings 6 (2 patties each), Calories 305, Fat 9.3g, Carbohydrates 47.7g, Protein 9.3g, Cholesterol 109mg, Sodium 218mg, Fiber 6.6g, Sugars 4.1g, WW Points 8

Servings 6, Calories 30, Carbohydrates 5.9g, Protein 1.1g, Cholesterol 0mg, Sodium 164mg, Sugars 3.0g

I love Mexican food, so it's only natural that these would be some of my favorite quinoa burgers!

Mexican Quinoa Burgers

Instructions:

1. If using flax eggs, combine 2 tablespoons ground flax seeds with 6 tablespoons warm water. Stir well and set aside. (Skip this step if you are using eggs.)

2. Spray a medium pan with olive oil and heat to medium. Add onion and pepper and cook for 10 to 12 minutes, until tender. Add garlic and cook for one more minute. Remove from heat and place in a large bowl.

3. In the bowl of a food processor, combine ¾ cup of the beans and ¾ cup of quinoa. Process until well blended. Add to the bowl with the onion mixture and stir in remaining beans and quinoa, cheese, taco seasoning, paprika, and salsa. Mix until combined and add in (flax) eggs and breadcrumbs. Mix well and allow to sit for 5 minutes. Form into patties and place the patties in the refrigerator for 30 minutes.

4. Heat oil to medium and cook until browned, flipping once.

1 medium onion, chopped
Olive oil spray
1 green or red pepper, chopped
4 cloves garlic, minced
1½ cups cooked black beans, drained and rinsed (1 can)
1½ cups cooked quinoa
½ cup cheddar or pepper jack cheese or Daiya shreds
2 tablespoons taco seasoning
1 teaspoon smoked paprika
2 tablespoons salsa
2 large eggs, beaten or flax eggs (2 tablespoons ground flax seeds + 6 tablespoons warm water)
1 cup gluten-free breadcrumbs
Coconut or canola oil, for cooking

{ Servings 6, Calories 234, Fat 4.2g, Carbohydrates 35.4g, Protein 13.6g, Cholesterol 64mg, Sodium 326mg, Fiber 7g, Sugars 4.1g }

I love wraps for lunch and this is one of my favorites! I especially like it with roasted red pepper hummus.

Mediterranean Quinoa Wrap

Instructions:

1. In a medium bowl combine quinoa, sun dried tomatoes, artichoke hearts, olives, lemon juice, and garlic.

2. Spread 1 ½ tablespoons of hummus on each tortilla. Add quinoa mixture and spinach and drizzle with balsamic vinegar. Wrap tightly, using toothpicks to secure if necessary. Cut in half and serve or wrap tightly in aluminum foil for later.

1 ½ cups cooked quinoa

8 sun dried tomatoes, rehydrated and chopped

1 cup water packed artichoke hearts, chopped

¼ cup olives, chopped

2 tablespoons lemon juice

2 cloves garlic, minced (less if you don't like raw garlic)

8 tablespoons hummus

4 gluten-free or whole-wheat wraps

1 cup baby spinach

4 teaspoons balsamic vinegar

Servings 4, Calories 264, Fat 8.7g, Carbohydrates 46g, Protein 10.6g, Cholesterol 0mg, Sodium 545mg, Fiber 12.2g, Sugars 0g

*Note that nutritional information uses a 111-calorie wrap.

Mains & Sides

This dish is a family favorite. I've even been known to serve it for casual entertaining. Even my parents—who prefer meat to meatless—enjoy this!

Smokey Quinoa Meatballs with Tomato Sauce

Instructions:

1. Heat a large saucepan to medium heat. Add tomatoes, olive oil, garlic, basil, sea salt, and black pepper. Simmer partially covered for 25 minutes. Add cream cheese and cook until melted, stirring occasionally.

2. Preheat oven to 400 degrees.

3. Meanwhile, if using chia egg in place of egg, combine chia seeds with 3 tablespoons warm water. Set aside. (Skip this step if you are using an egg.)

4. Spray a large skillet with 1 tablespoon olive oil and heat to medium. Add onion and cook for 12 to 14 minutes, until tender. Add garlic and cook for one minute longer. Remove from heat and allow to cool slightly.

5. Place quinoa, garbanzo beans, sun dried tomatoes, and sunflower seeds in your food processor. Pulse until well combined. (Do not overprocess, you want some of the texture from the sunflower seeds and sundried tomatoes to remain.)

6. Transfer to a bowl and stir in onion mixture, parsley, basil, oregano, garlic, 1 tablespoon olive oil, soy sauce, liquid smoke, and (chia) egg.

7. Using a teaspoon measure, shape into small balls and place on a parchment-lined baking sheet. Brush with remaining 1 tablespoon of olive oil. Bake for 10 minutes. Turn balls and bake for 10 more minutes.

8. Meanwhile, cook pasta according to package directions. Drain, and divide between 8 serving bowls. Top with meatballs and sauce.

{ Servings 8, Calories 463, Fat 18.6g, Carbohydrates 651.g, Protein 10.9g, Cholesterol 27mg, Sodium 449mg, Fiber 7g, Sugars 6g }

28 ounces diced tomatoes

¼ cup olive oil

6–10 cloves garlic, minced (more or less to taste)

1 tablespoon dried basil or ¼ cup fresh chopped basil

¾ teaspoon sea salt

½ teaspoon fresh ground black pepper

½ cup cream cheese–low fat dairy or nondairy

1 egg or 1 chia egg (1 tablespoon chia seeds plus 3 tablespoons water)

1 large onion, chopped fine

1 teaspoon minced garlic

1 cup cooked quinoa

1 cup garbanzo beans

½ cup finely chopped sun dried tomatoes, rehydrated

½ cup sunflower seeds

¼ cup fresh parsley or 1 tablespoon dried

¼ cup fresh basil or 1 tablespoon dried

1 tablespoon fresh oregano or 1 teaspoon dried

3 tablespoons olive oil, divided

2 teaspoons gluten-free tamari

2 teaspoons liquid smoke

16 ounces quinoa linguine

Although this recipe is a bit involved, it really isn't fussy. If your poblano peppers tear in the peeling process, don't worry! The breading will cover it up. The filling and sauce can be made a day ahead of time and reheated. Additionally, the peppers can be stuffed and breaded up to 3 hours ahead of time.

Baked Chile Rellenos

Instructions:

1. Place oven rack in the top position and turn to broil. Place a sheet of aluminum foil on the rack below. Place chilies on the top rack and broil until blackened, turning carefully with tongs so that all sides blacken. Place in a covered container for 15 minutes. Peel chilies. Slit down the middle and remove seeds.

2. Meanwhile, spray a skillet with olive oil and heat to medium. Add onion and red pepper. Cook for 8 minutes. Add garlic and cook for 30 seconds, or until fragrant. Add corn, quinoa, paprika, and cumin. Cook for 3 more minutes. Reduce heat to low. Stir in cilantro, cream cheese and pepper jack. Cook until the cheeses are melted. Remove from heat and allow to cool slightly. (This is a good time to start the sauce.)

3. Preheat oven to 425 degrees. Line a baking sheet with parchment paper and spray with olive oil.

4. Stuff each chili with the quinoa mixture. Use 2 to 3 toothpicks to secure.

5. In a shallow dish combine the corn flour and quinoa flour. Combine milk and lemon juice and place in a shallow dish. Make breading by combining quinoa flakes and rice crackers in a food processor until smooth. Transfer to a shallow dish.

6. Dip chilies in the flour and then in the milk/lemon juice mixture. Coat with bread crumbs and place on prepared baking sheet. Spray liberally with olive oil spray. Bake for 25 to 35 minutes, until brown. Serve with sauce. (Reserve remaining sauce for another use.)

To make sauce:

Spray a saucepan with olive oil and heat to medium. Add onion and cook for 10 to 12 minutes. Add garlic and sauté for 30 seconds to 1 minute, until fragrant. Add tomatoes, chopped chipotle chile, oregano, salt, and pepper. Reduce to low and cook covered for 30 minutes.

{ *Note: If you have a corn allergy, substitute any gluten-free flour for the corn flour and skip the frozen corn.

Note that nutritional information uses half of the sauce.

Servings 6, Calories 465, Fat 14.9g, Carbohydrates 68.6g, Protein 19.5g, Cholesterol 34mg, Sodium 992mg, Fiber 12.7g, Sugars 3.8g }

6 poblano peppers
1 cup chopped onion
½ cup red pepper, chopped
2 teaspoons minced garlic
½ cup frozen corn, thawed
1 cup cooked quinoa
1 teaspoon smoked paprika
1 teaspoon ground cumin
¼ cup cilantro, chopped
4 ounces cream cheese, dairy or nondairy
½ cup shredded pepper jack, dairy or nondairy

Breading
Flour Mixture
⅓ cup fine corn flour*
½ cup toasted quinoa flour (or gluten-free flour of choice)

Milk Mixture
1 cup unsweetened almond milk (or milk of choice)
2 teaspoons lemon juice

Crumbs
1 cup quinoa flakes
1½ cups rice crackers

Sauce
1 cup chopped onion
1 teaspoon minced garlic
128-ounce can crushed tomatoes
1 chipotle chile in adobo sauce, chopped
1 teaspoon Mexican oregano
1 teaspoon sea salt
½ teaspoon fresh ground pepper

I rarely make soup and when I do I want it to be packed with flavor. This soup delivers on flavor and also scores big on nutrition. It's packed with vitamin C, manganese, vitamin A and phosphorous.

Broccoli Spinach Quinoa Soup

Instructions:

1. Heat olive oil in a large stock pan. Add onion, salt, and pepper and cook for 10 to 12 minutes, until tender. Add quinoa and garlic and stir for 1 to 2 minutes. Add in vegetable broth, broccoli, and potato. Bring to a simmer and reduce heat to low. Cover and cook for 35 minutes. Remove cover and add spinach, tahini, salt, and peppers. Cook until spinach is wilted.

2. Remove from heat and allow to cool. When cool enough to handle, transfer to a blender and puree in batches. (If you want a thinner soup you can add additional vegetable broth.) Return to the pan and heat to low, add cheese and cook until melted.

2 tablespoons olive oil
1 red onion, chopped fine
1 teaspoon sea salt
½ teaspoon black pepper
1 cup quinoa, rinsed
2 teaspoons minced garlic
6 cups vegetable broth
5 cups chopped broccoli
1 russet potato, peeled and chopped
6 ounces spinach
2 tablespoons tahini
1 teaspoon sea salt (more or less to taste)
½ teaspoon fresh ground black pepper
⅛ teaspoon cayenne pepper
1 cup sharp cheddar cheese or Daiya cheddar shreds

Servings 10, Calories 212, Fat 10.3g, Carbohydrates 19.7g, Protein 11.4g, Cholesterol 12mg, Sodium 1010mg, Fiber 3.7g, Sugars 2g

The holidays just wouldn't be the same without stuffing! This dish pleases the meat eaters and vegans alike.

Bread, Quinoa & Cranberry Stuffing

Instructions:

1. Preheat oven to 250 degrees. Place cubed bread on a rimmed baking sheet. Bake for 1 hour, stirring occasionally. Transfer to a large bowl. Toss with cooked quinoa, cranberries, and pecan halves.

2. Meanwhile, heat olive oil in a large skillet. Add onions and cook for 8 minutes. Add celery and cook for 5 minutes more. Add garlic, thyme, sage, parsley, salt, and pepper and cook for 1 more minute. Transfer to bowl with bread and toss well.

3. Preheat oven to 350 degrees.

4. Return the skillet to the stove and heat to medium low. Add milk and butter and bring to a simmer, stirring occasionally. Cook for 2 minutes and then add milk mixture to stuffing. Season to taste with salt and pepper.

5. Transfer to a baking dish and bake for 30 minutes. If desired, top with gravy.

1 pound gluten-free bread, cubed
2 cups cooked quinoa
1 cup dried cranberries
1 cup pecans, chopped
1½ tablespoons olive oil
3 medium yellow onions, chopped
5 stalks celery, chopped
8 cloves garlic, minced
2 tablespoons chopped fresh thyme (or 2 teaspoons dried)
1 tablespoon chopped fresh sage (or 1 teaspoon dried)
½ cup fresh parsley, chopped (or 3 tablespoons dried)
1 teaspoon sea salt
½ teaspoon fresh ground black pepper
1 cup unsweetened almond milk or milk of choice
1 tablespoon Earth Balance or butter
Salt and pepper to taste

Servings 12, Calories 232, Fat 11.4g, Carbohydrates 27.8g, Protein 7.7g, Cholesterol 3mg, Sodium 366mg, Fiber 5.5g, Sugars 11.1g

This has become one of my favorite make-ahead dishes. I typically double the recipe and put a casserole in the freezer!

Broccoli Quinoa Casserole

Instructions:

1. Preheat oven to 350 degrees.

2. Toss together broccoli and quinoa in a large bowl. Add cream of celery soup, ground mustard, cayenne pepper and ¾ cup of shredded cheese. Toss well and transfer to a 13 x 9 baking dish. Top with remaining ¾ cup of cheese and bake for 40 to 45 minutes.

3. **Make Ahead:** This dish may be made ahead and frozen prior to baking. If making ahead, steam the broccoli for 8 minutes prior to tossing with the quinoa. (This will preserve the color when frozen.) Allow the casserole to thaw out overnight in the refrigerator and bake for 45 minutes.

Cream of Celery Soup

Makes 2 cups, may be doubled or tripled and frozen

1. Heat olive oil over medium heat. Add in flour and whisk. Cook for 2 to 3 minutes, until the mixture bubbles and begins to brown. Whisk in almond milk and vegetable broth. Cook, whisking frequently, for 5 to 7 minutes or until the mixture begins to thicken.

2. Stir in the celery, Parmesan cheese, onion powder, smoked paprika, sea salt, and pepper. Simmer for 6 to 8 minutes. Allow to cool to use in a recipe or freeze in 2-cup portions for later use.

Servings 8, Calories 254, Fat 15g, Carbohydrates 19.7g, Protein 11.6g, Cholesterol 23mg, Sodium 522mg, Fiber 3.4g, Sugars 1.4g

5 cups chopped broccoli

3 cups cooked quinoa (about 1 cup uncooked)

2 cups cream of celery soup (see below)

½ teaspoon ground mustard

¼ teaspoon cayenne pepper

1 ½ cups sharp cheddar cheese or Daiya shreds, divided

Cream of Celery Soup

3 tablespoons extra virgin olive oil (or butter)

¼ cup toasted quinoa flour (or flour of choice)

1 cup unsweetened almond milk (or milk of choice)

1 cup vegetable broth

¼ cup finely chopped celery

2 tablespoons Parmesan cheese (or vegan Parmesan)

½ teaspoon onion powder

¼ teaspoon smoked paprika

1 teaspoon sea salt

¼ teaspoon fresh ground black pepper

I love the sweet heat of these potatoes. They may be prepared a day ahead of time then topped and baked just prior to serving.

Twice-Baked Sweet Potatoes

Instructions:

1. Preheat oven to 375 degrees. Line a rimmed baking sheet with parchment paper.

2. Pierce the sweet potatoes with a fork. Bake until tender—between 40 and 55 minutes depending on the size. (Larger potatoes could take a little longer. You will know your potatoes are done when they are tender when pierced at the thickest part.)

3. Allow the potatoes to cool until they are cool enough to handle and then cut them in half lengthwise. Scoop out the flesh, leaving 1/4 inch in the shells. Place the flesh in a bowl and mash with the sour cream and milk, using a potato masher or fork. Stir in cooked quinoa, maple syrup, garlic, sage, cayenne pepper, white pepper, and sea salt.

4. Place filled potatoes on prepared baking sheet and top with cheese and pecans. Bake for 15 minutes, until cheese is melted and bubbly.
Turn the broiler on for the last 2 to 3 minutes if desired.

4 small sweet potatoes (about 2 pounds)
2 tablespoons almond milk (or milk of choice)
1/2 cup dairy or nondairy sour cream
1 cup cooked quinoa
1 tablespoon maple syrup
2 cloves garlic, minced
1 teaspoon chopped fresh sage or 1/4 teaspoon dried
1/4 teaspoon cayenne pepper (optional)
1/4 teaspoon white pepper
1/2 teaspoon sea salt
1/4 cup grated mozzarella cheese or Daiya mozzarella
1/4 cup pecans, toasted and chopped

Servings 8, Calories 229, Fat 6.5g, Carbohydrates 39.3g, Protein 4.4g, Cholesterol 9mg, Sodium 157mg, Fiber 5.6g, Sugars 2.4g

I love this "pizza" as written, but it is also great topped with pesto and roasted vegetables for a cheese- and flour-free pizza that is so delicious it will surprise you!

Potato & Quinoa Crusted Pizza

Instructions:

1. Preheat oven to 375. Line 2 prepared pie plates with parchment paper. If using flax egg, combine ground flax seeds with warm water and set aside. (Skip this step if you are using eggs.)

2. Using a box grater or food processor, grate potatoes and then place in salted water for at least 15 minutes. Using a clean dish towel, ring the water out of the potatoes. Place in a large bowl and add quinoa, nutritional yeast, Italian seasoning, and salt.

3. Spread quinoa and potato mixture on 2 prepared pie plates to ⅛ inch thick. Bake for 25 to 30 minutes.

4. Remove from oven. Spread pesto or marinara on crust. Top with cheese and remaining toppings. Bake for 20 more minutes. (Optional: for a crispier crust, remove crust from pie plate and place on a pizza peel. Top and bake directly on a pizza stone.)

1 ½ pounds white potatoes, scrubbed well

2 cups cooked quinoa

2 eggs , beaten or flax eggs (2 tablespoons ground flax seeds + 6 tablespoons warm water)

2 tablespoons nutritional yeast

2 teaspoons Italian seasoning

1 teaspoon sea salt

Optional Toppings:

⅔ cup gluten-free marinara or pesto

¾ cup mozzarella cheese or Daiya mozzarella

1 roasted red pepper, diced

½ red onion, sliced thin

⅓ cup black olives

Crust Only
Servings 8 (1/4 pie), Calories 122, Fat 1.4g, Carbohydrates 23.2, Protein 4.9g, Cholesterol 1mg, Sodium 248mg, Fiber 3.6g, Sugars 1.1g

This is one of those healthy eating dishes that feels rather indulgent. I like to cut a sprouted corn tortilla into strips and toast it until it is crunchy and then sprinkle it on top for a little extra texture!

Quinoa Burrito Bowls

Instructions:

1. Bring lime juice, red wine vinegar, water, maple syrup, and salt to a boil in a small saucepan. Add onions and cook for 1 minute, stirring to make sure onions are covered. Remove from heat and transfer to a bowl. Allow to cool slightly and then refrigerate until ready to use. (The onions may be made ahead and refrigerated. I like to make extra to have on hand for salads, wraps, and sandwiches.)

2. Meanwhile, bring quinoa, vegetable broth, sea salt, and cayenne pepper to a simmer. Reduce to low and cover. Cook for 30 to 35 minutes. Remove from heat. Stir in cilantro, jalapeño, lime juice and black beans, corn, and red pepper and allow to sit covered for 5 minutes.

3. Place mixture in a bowl and add tomato and pickled onions. Top with salsa, guacamole and/or Greek yogurt (optional).

Pickled Onions

¼ cup lime juice
¼ cup red wine vinegar
¼ cup water
1 tablespoon maple syrup
¼ teaspoon salt
1 large red onion, sliced

Quinoa

1 cup quinoa, rinsed
1 ¼ cups vegetable broth
½ teaspoon sea salt
¼ teaspoon cayenne pepper
½ cup cilantro, chopped
1 jalapeño, chopped
2 tablespoons lime juice
3 cups black beans
    (about 2 cans)
1 cup fresh or thawed
    frozen corn
1 cup roasted red pepper,
    diced
½ cup grape tomatoes,
    chopped
For Topping: salsa, guacamole
    or Greek yogurt

Servings 6, Calories 275, Fat 2.4g, Carbohydrates 49.7g, Protein 15g, Cholesterol 0mg, Sodium 579mg, Fiber 12.5g, Sugars 7.9g

This is a fun dish that could be made even heartier with the addition of sausage. I like vegan Field Roast, but any sausage you like will work!

Quinoa Paella

Instructions:

1. Heat olive oil in a large skillet or paella pan. Add onion and cook for 5 minutes.

2. Add broccoli and red pepper and cook for 5 more minutes.

3. Add in garlic, quinoa, saffron threads, turmeric, red pepper flakes, paprika, sea salt, lemon juice, and tomatoes. Cook for 3 minutes, stirring well so that everything is combined.

4. Add vegetable broth and bring to a simmer. Cover and reduce heat to low. Cook for 20 minutes.

5. Add in peas and artichoke hearts and cook for 10 more minutes. Remove from heat and allow to sit covered for 5 to 10 more minutes.

1 tablespoon extra virgin olive oil

1 onion, chopped

2 cups broccoli florets

1 red bell pepper, seeded and chopped

4 garlic cloves, minced

1 cup quinoa, rinsed

¼ teaspoon saffron threads

1 teaspoon turmeric

¼ teaspoon red pepper flakes

1½ teaspoons paprika

½ teaspoon sea salt

1 tablespoon lemon juice

2 tomatoes, skinned and cut into cubes

1½ cups gluten-free vegetable broth

1 cup baby peas, thawed

14½ ounces water-packed artichoke hearts

Servings 6, Calories 223, Fat 4.8g, Carbohydrates 36.4g, Protein 10.7g, Cholesterol 0mg, Sodium 797mg, Fiber 8.2g, Sugars 4.75g

This dish is perfect for the holidays!

Stuffed Butternut Squash

Instructions:

1. Preheat oven to 425 degrees. Spray a baking dish with olive oil and place squash halves cut side down in the dish. Bake for 45 to 65 minutes, until tender. (The larger the squash, the longer it will take.) Allow to cool slightly. When cool enough to handle, scoop out pulp leaving ½-inch shell.

2. Meanwhile, spray a skillet with olive oil and heat to medium. Add onion and cook for 10 to 12 minutes, until tender. Add garlic and quinoa and cook for 1 minute more. Transfer mixture to a medium bowl and stir in squash pulp, apple, cranberries, sour cream, sage, paprika, salt, and pepper. Divide mixture among squash shells. Place on a rimmed baking sheet and sprinkle with cheese and pine nuts. Bake for 15 minutes. Serve warm.

2 medium butternut squash, halved and seeded
1 onion, chopped fine
3 cloves garlic, minced
1½ cups cooked quinoa
1 Granny Smith apple, peeled, cored and grated
⅓ cup dried cranberries
1 cup vegan or low fat sour cream or Greek yogurt
½ teaspoon dried sage
½ teaspoon smoked paprika
1 teaspoon sea salt
½ teaspoon fresh ground black pepper
½ cup goat cheese, cheddar cheese or cheddar style Daiya
½ cup pine nuts

Servings 8, Calories 291, Fat 13.3g, Carbohydrates 40.8g, Protein 7.8g, Cholesterol 14mg, Sodium 393mg, Fiber 6.6g, Sugars 8.5g

This dish is a favorite around our house. In fact, it is one of my husband's favorite quinoa recipes! He likes it with a little goat cheese on top and I think it is heavenly as is.

Quinoa with Sausage, Pears & Candied Pecans

Instructions:

1. Heat olive oil over medium heat in a skillet. Remove casings from sausage and slice. Cook for 8 to 10 minutes breaking up slices with a large spoon. Remove from pan with a slotted spoon and place on a towel lined plate.

2. Add onion and ½ teaspoon of salt and cook for 8 minutes or until onion is slightly tender. Add sherry to the pan and scrape up browned bits. Cook for 1 to 2 minutes, until the sherry has evaporated.

3. Add in the quinoa, sage, thyme, parsley and bay leaf. Bring to a simmer and then reduce to low. Cover and cook for 30 minutes.

4. Return the sausage to the pan and add in pears. Cook for 2 minutes and remove from heat. Cover and allow to sit for 5 minutes. Remove bay leaf from mixture. Top with walnuts and serve.

5. Make the candied pecans while the quinoa is cooking. To do so, first melt butter over medium heat. Add pecans and cook for 2 minutes, until lightly toasted. Add sugar and cook for 1 more minute or until the sugar is melted. Add a pinch of salt and remove from heat.

{ Servings 8, Calories 288, Fat 10.7g, Carbohydrates 27.9g, Protein 16.2g, Cholesterol 2mg, Sodium 288mg, Fiber 4.8g, Sugars 7.2g }

1 tablespoon olive oil
12 ounces gluten-free vegan chorizo or Italian sausage
1 cup chopped onion
2 tablespoon dry sherry
1 cup quinoa, rinsed
1 tablespoon fresh sage, chopped (or 1 teaspoon dried)
1 teaspoon fresh thyme, chopped (or ¼ teaspoon dried)
3 tablespoons fresh parsley, chopped (or 1 tablespoon dried)
1 bay leaf
2 small ripe pears peeled and cut into ½-inch pieces

Candied Pecans

½ tablespoon Earth Balance or unsalted butter
¼ cup pecans, chopped
1 tablespoon coconut palm sugar
Sea salt and freshly ground black pepper

I'll be honest—this recipe surprised me. I never make anything that I don't think I will like but I was completely blown away by just how much I loved this. Family members swear that goat cheese takes this to the next level.

Quinoa Pilaf Amandine

Instructions:

1. Bring water to boil in a medium pot. Add green beans and cook for 3 minutes. Drain and place in a bath of ice water. Drain and set aside.

2. Meanwhile, add olive oil to another pot and heat over medium heat. Add onion and celery and cook for 8 minutes. Add garlic and quinoa and cook for 2 more minutes, stirring occasionally. Add vegetable broth, bay leaf, sea salt, black pepper, and cayenne pepper. Bring to a simmer and reduce to low. Cover and cook 30 to 35 minutes. Remove from heat and stir in lemon juice and green beans. Cover and allow to sit for 10 minutes. Top with almonds and serve warm.

8 ounces green beans, trimmed and cut into 1-inch pieces

1 tablespoon olive oil

½ cup chopped onion

½ cup chopped celery

3 cloves garlic, minced

1 cup quinoa, rinsed

1 ¼ cup vegetable broth

1 bay leaf

½ teaspoon sea salt

½ teaspoon ground black pepper

⅛ teaspoon cayenne pepper

1 teaspoon lemon juice

⅓ cup slivered almonds, toasted

Optional: goat cheese, cheddar cheese, or nut cheese for topping

Servings 6, Calories 177, Fat 7g, Carbohydrates 23 g, Protein 6.9g, Cholesterol 0mg, Sodium 327mg, Fiber 4.2g, Sugars 1.5g

This may seem like an unusual combination at first, but I urge you to give it a try! As one (Italian) tester said, "It came out like a nice, full-bodied meat sauce....I ate the leftovers cold, right out of the fridge Yes. It was THAT good."

Quinoa & Spaghetti

Instructions:

1. Cook pasta according to package directions. Drain and toss with olive oil if desired.

2. Meanwhile, spray a large saucepan with olive oil spray. Add onion and cook for 8 to 10 minutes, until tender. Add quinoa, garlic, oregano, red pepper, black pepper and sea salt. Cook for 3 to 4 minutes, stirring constantly. Add marinara, vegetable broth, olives, sherry, and capers. Bring to a simmer. Cover and reduce to low. Cook covered for 30 minutes. Remove from heat and allow to sit covered for another 5 minutes.

3. Divide pasta among 4 plates. Top with sauce and garnish with parsley and additional olives.

8 ounces quinoa spaghetti

Olive oil spray

1 large white or yellow onion, chopped

¾ cup red or rainbow quinoa, rinsed

6 cloves garlic, minced

1 teaspoon dried oregano

½ teaspoon crushed red pepper

¼ teaspoon fresh ground black pepper

½ teaspoon sea salt

2 cups marinara

¾ cup vegetable broth

½ cup black or pimento stuffed olives

¼ cup dry sherry

1 tablespoon capers

Servings 4, Calories 372, Fat 5.2g, Carbohydrates 67.1g, Protein 11g, Cholesterol 0mg, Sodium 598mg, Fiber 6.2g, Sugars 6.3g

I can't think of a better way to start a holiday meal than a flavorful soup! I like to top this with a dollop of yogurt or sour cream and chopped pistachios.

Curried Butternut Squash & Quinoa Soup

Instructions:

1. Spray a large saucepan with olive oil and add chopped onion. Cook for 8 to 10 minutes, until tender. Add quinoa, garlic, sea salt, curry powder, cumin, and cayenne pepper. Cook for 4 to 5 minutes, stirring often. Add in vegetable broth and squash and bring to a simmer. Reduce to low and cover. Cook for 35 minutes. Remove from heat and allow to sit covered for 5 minutes. Remove lid and allow to cool slightly.

2. Puree soup with an immersion blender. Alternatively, working in batches puree soup in your blender. Salt and pepper to taste and serve with a dollop of soy or dairy yogurt if desired.

Olive oil spray

1 yellow or white onion, chopped

1 cup quinoa, rinsed

6 cloves garlic, minced

¾ teaspoon sea salt

1½ tablespoons curry powder

½ tablespoon ground cumin

¼ teaspoon cayenne pepper, optional

6 cups vegetable broth

2½ lb butternut squash, peeled, seeded and diced

Greek yogurt, for topping (optional)

Servings 8, Calories 181, Fat 2.7g, Carbohydrates 33g, Protein 8.4g, Cholesterol 0mg, Sodium 757mg, Fiber 5g, Sugars 4.3g

As a busy mom, one-skillet meals are a lifesaver!

Chicken Quinoa & Spinach Skillet

Instructions:

1. Spray a large skillet with olive oil and heat to medium. Cook chicken or tempeh until golden brown. Remove from pan.

2. Spray skillet with olive oil again. Add onion and cook for 10 minutes, until tender. Add garlic, quinoa, sea salt, and red pepper and cook for 3 minutes longer. Add vegetable broth, tomatoes, tomato paste, and nutritional yeast to the skillet. Cook over for 2 minutes.

3. Return chicken to the skillet and stir in spinach. Cook until wilted. Salt and pepper to taste. Top with cheese if desired and serve warm.

Olive oil spray

10 ounces chicken or tempeh

1 onion, chopped fine

3 cloves garlic, minced

3 cups cooked quinoa

½ teaspoon sea salt

½ teaspoon crushed
    red pepper (optional)

½ cup vegetable broth

2 cups chopped tomatoes

1 tablespoon tomato paste

¼ cup nutritional yeast
    (optional)

3 cups baby spinach

Optional Toppings:

¾ cup vegan feta, feta, or
    Daiya cheddar

{
With Chicken
Servings 6, Calories 331, Fat 5.6g, Carbohydrates 38.3g, Protein 33.3g, Cholesterol 55mg, Sodium 409mg, Fiber 7.4g, Sugars 3.8g
With Tempeh
Servings 6, Calories 361, Fat 11.1g, Carbohydrates 44 g, Protein 25.9g, Cholesterol 0mg, Sodium 371mg, Fiber 7.4g, Sugars 3.8g
}

This healthy and hearty casserole is great for company! It can be made up to one day ahead.

Caramelized Onion, Quinoa & White Bean Casserole

Instructions:

1. Preheat oven to 400 degrees. Spray a 2 ½-quart baking dish with olive oil.

2. Heat oil to medium high in a Dutch oven. Add onions and salt and cook for about 7 minutes, stirring occasionally. Reduce heat to medium low and cook for 20 minutes. Add balsamic vinegar and cook for 5 minutes more. Stir in garlic and red pepper flakes and cook until fragrant. Add wine and cook for about 1 minute, scraping the bottom of the pan. Remove onions from heat and place in the prepared pan. (Leave any wine that hasn't cooked off in the pan.)

3. Add the cannellini beans, quinoa, vegetable broth, and rosemary to the same Dutch oven. Bring to a simmer. Stir in ¼ cup of cheese and cream cheese. Stir until well combined. Season to taste with salt and pepper and place the mixture over the onions in the baking dish. Top with remaining ½ cup of cheese and sprinkle with crushed red pepper flakes and fresh ground black pepper if desired.

4. Bake for 20 to 25 minutes. Allow to cool slightly before serving.

1 tablespoon extra virgin olive oil

3 onions, peeled and sliced thin

½ teaspoon sea salt

1 tablespoon balsamic vinegar

2 teaspoons minced garlic

¼ teaspoon red pepper flakes

½ cup white wine

3 cups cannellini beans, drained and rinsed (about 2 cans)

3 cups cooked quinoa

1 cup of vegetable broth

1 teaspoon fresh rosemary, minced

¾ cup grated white cheddar or Daiya, divided

½ cup nondairy or low fat cream cheese

Calories 349, Fat 7.5g, Carbohydrates 49.1g, Protein 16.6g, Cholesterol 2mg, Sodium 63.3 mg, Fiber 13.4 g, Sugars 3.7g.

Note: Sodium may be reduced by cooking dried beans

This side dish is packed with flavor! It holds well for a couple of days and may be made ahead and reheated.

Sun Dried Tomato Pesto Quinoa

Instructions:

1. In a blender or food processor, combine sun dried tomatoes, walnuts, garlic, basil, olive oil, water, sea salt, and fresh ground pepper. Process until smooth.

2. Place quinoa in a medium bowl and toss with pesto. Top with olive and sprinkle with parsley.

½ cup sun dried tomatoes, rehydrated

⅓ cup walnuts

3 cloves garlic, minced

½ cup fresh basil, copped

⅓ cup extra virgin olive oil

½ cup water

1 teaspoon sea salt

½ teaspoon fresh ground pepper

2½ cups cooked quinoa

2 tablespoons chopped olives

Parsley, for garnish

{ Servings 6, Calories 242, Fat 18.2g, Carbohydrates 17.2g, Protein 5.3g, Cholesterol 0mg, Sodium 363mg, Fiber 2.7g }

This hearty dish is perfect for cooler weather. Preparing the rolls seems like a lot of work, but it is worth the effort!

Quinoa Cabbage Rolls

Instructions:

1. Remove the core from the cabbage. Bring a large pot of salted water to a boil. Cover and cook cabbage for 8 to 10 minutes. Place in cold water. Peel 12 leaves for the rolls, cutting the thick vein from the leaves as necessary. Drain on towels.

2. Preheat oven to 375 degrees.

3. Meanwhile, spray a medium saucepan with olive oil. Add onion and pepper and cook for 10 to 12 minutes, until tender. Add quinoa, garlic, and tomato paste and sauté for 2 minutes. Add vegetable broth, parsley, thyme, salt, and pepper. Bring to a simmer and reduce heat to low. Cover and cook for 30 to 35 minutes. Stir in zucchini and Parmesan cheese and re-cover. Allow to sit off the heat for 5 minutes. Cool slightly and stir in egg if desired. (You want to make sure the mixture has cooled enough to not cook your egg.)

4. Divide quinoa mixture among the prepared cabbage leaves. Roll up leaves to enclose the filling. Place seam-side down in a casserole pan. Top with tomato sauce.

5. Bake for 30 to 35 minutes. Allow to sit for 10 minutes and serve.

1 head of cabbage
Olive oil spray
1 onion, diced
1 red pepper, chopped
1 cup quinoa, rinsed
1 teaspoon garlic, minced
2 tablespoons tomato paste
1 1/2 cups vegetable broth
2 teaspoons dried parsley (or 2 tablespoons fresh)
1/2 teaspoon dried thyme
1/2 teaspoon sea salt
1/4 teaspoon fresh ground black pepper
1 cup diced zucchini
1/3 cup grated Parmesan cheese or vegan Parmesan
1 egg, beaten (optional)
2 cups tomato sauce

Servings 6, Calories 214, Fat 4.7g, Carbohydrates 33.8g, Protein 11.6g, Cholesterol 32mg, Sodium 902mg, Fiber 7.3g, Sugars 10.2g

I love the kick that curry powder gives this pilaf, but if you aren't a fan, try using Thai curry. It has a milder kick but still packs a ton of flavor.

Curried Quinoa & Sweet Potato Pilaf

Instructions:

1. Spray a medium saucepan with olive oil. Add onion and cook for 8 to 10 minutes, until tender.

2. Add quinoa, garlic, curry powder, cumin, and sea salt. Cook for 4 minutes, stirring occasionally.

3. Add sweet potato and vegetable broth and bring to a simmer. Reduce heat to low and cover. Cook for 30 minutes.

4. Stir in apples, peas, and currants and re-cover. Cook for 5 more minutes then remove from heat. Allow to sit covered for 5 minutes. Top with walnuts and serve warm.

Olive oil spray
1 small onion, chopped
1 cup quinoa, rinsed
2 cloves garlic, minced
1 ½ teaspoons curry powder
½ teaspoon ground cumin
½ teaspoon sea salt
1 sweet potato, peeled and
    diced
1 ½ cups vegetable broth
2 Granny Smith apples, peeled
    and cubed
½ cup frozen green peas
2 tablespoon currants, raisins or
    dried cranberries
2 tablespoons chopped
    walnuts, toasted

Servings 6, Calories 192, Fat 3.8g, Carbohydrates 33.7g, Protein 7.1g, Cholesterol 0mg, Sodium 357mg, Fat 5.3g, Sugars 9.1g

No special occasion would be the same in my house without a little hint of Mexican food! This is actually fantastic alongside more traditional holiday fare. Don't know what to do with the leftovers? I love this as a unique taco filling!

Quinoa Cornbread Stuffing

Instructions:

1. Preheat oven to 350 degrees. Spray a small casserole dish with olive oil.

2. Spray a large skillet well with canola oil and heat to medium high. Add chorizo and cook for 5 to 7 minutes, breaking up chorizo with the back of your fork. Reduce heat to medium and add onion, poblano pepper, celery, and carrot and cook until tender, about 10 more minutes. Add garlic and cook for 1 minute longer. Stir in crumbled cornbread, quinoa, cilantro, salt, and pepper. Add vegetable broth and mix gently until well combined.

3. Transfer to prepared casserole dish and dot with butter. Bake for 20 minutes. Garnish with additional cilantro if desired.

8 ounces gluten-free chorizo (I use vegan)
2 cups chopped red onion
1 poblano pepper, seeded and chopped
2 celery stalks, chopped
1 carrot, peeled and chopped
4 cloves garlic, minced
2 cups crumbled gluten-free cornbread
1 cup cooked quinoa
¼ cup cilantro, chopped
1 teaspoon sea salt
¼ teaspoon fresh ground black pepper
½ cup vegetable broth
1 tablespoon Earth Balance or unsalted butter

Servings 6, Calories 251, Fat 11.7g, Carbohydrates 29g, Protein 9.4g, Cholesterol 22mg, Sodium 927mg, Fiber 10.8g, Sugars 4.1g

This is an elegant gluten-free side dish that also works great as a vegetarian main!

Arugula Quinoa Risotto with Ricotta & Walnuts

Instructions:

1. Put vegetable broth in a medium pan and warm.

2. In a separate pan, heat the olive oil to medium. Add onion and cook for 10 to 12 minutes, until tender. Add quinoa, garlic, thyme, and salt and cook for 3 minutes, stirring well. Add wine or broth and cook until it is almost absorbed.

3. Add the warm broth by the ½-cup full, cooking until the liquid is absorbed before adding more. Cook over medium low until all the broth has been incorporated. Stir in the lemon juice, arugula, and Parmesan and cook until the arugula is wilted.

4. Divide into serving bowls and top with ricotta and walnuts.

1½ cups vegetable broth
2 tablespoons extra virgin olive oil
1 onion, chopped
1 cups quinoa, rinsed
2 cloves garlic, minced
½ teaspoon dried thyme
⅓ teaspoon sea salt
½ cup white wine or vegetable broth
2 tablespoons lemon juice
2 cups chopped arugula
½ cup grated Parmesan or vegan Parmesan
½ cup or tofu ricotta
6 tablespoons walnuts, toasted and chopped

Servings 6, Calories 280, Fat 14.5g, Carbohydrates 22.7g, Protein 12.2g, Cholesterol 12mg, Sodium 498mg, Fiber 2.9g, Sugars 2.5g

The holidays just wouldn't be the same without sweet potato casserole. Here is a healthier and gluten-free version of a classic!

Sweet Potato Casserole with Crumbly Quinoa Topping

Instructions:

1. Preheat oven to 375 degrees. Rinse potatoes and bake for 45 minutes, or until tender. Allow to cool slightly and then cut open and scoop the flesh out into a large bowl.

2. Add maple syrup, milk, butter, vanilla, and cinnamon to the bowl. Mash with a potato masher and transfer mixture to a casserole dish.

3. In a separate bowl, combine quinoa, pecans, flour and palm sugar. Combine with a fork and add butter. Mix with a pastry cutter or fork until a crumble forms. Sprinkle topping over sweet potatoes.

4. Bake for 30 to 35 minutes.

1 ½ pounds sweet potato
⅓ cup maple syrup
1 cup almond milk or milk of choice
2 tablespoons Earth Balance or unsalted butter
1 teaspoon vanilla extract
½ teaspoon ground cinnamon

Topping
½ cup cooked quinoa
½ cup chopped pecans
½ cup all purpose gluten-free quinoa flour blend
⅓ cup coconut palm sugar (or sweetener of choice)
4 tablespoons Earth Balance or unsalted butter, room temperature

Servings 12, Fat 14.1g, Carbohydrates 34.2g, Protein 2.6g, Cholesterol 15mg, Sodium 62mg, Fiber 3.5g, Sugars 10.4g

This is a healthier version of an old favorite!

Quinoa Casserole with Broccoli & Cheese

Instructions:

1. Preheat oven to 350 degrees.

2. Heat olive oil over medium heat in a large oven safe skillet. Add onion and cook for 8 minutes, or until tender. Add garlic and cook for 1 more minute. Add broccoli and quinoa and cook for 4 minutes. Remove from heat.

3. Meanwhile, heat butter over medium heat. Whisk in flour and cook for 3 minutes. Add ½ cup of milk and whisk until well combined. Add in remaining milk. Whisk until boiling and thickened, about 7 minutes. Reduce heat to low and add cream cheese and cheese. Cook until melted and stir in nutritional yeast (optional), garlic powder, turmeric, salt, and pepper. Pour over quinoa mixture and stir until well combined. (If you don't have a large oven safe skilled simply transfer to a casserole dish.) If desired, top with additional cheese.

4. Bake for 30 to 35 minutes. Allow to cool slightly and serve warm.

1 tablespoon olive oil
1 large onion, chopped
3 cloves garlic, minced
3 cups chopped broccoli
3 cups cooked quinoa
3 tablespoons Earth Balance or butter
3 tablespoons all purpose flour or gluten-free flour blend
2½ cups unsweetened soy or low fat milk
½ cup nondairy or dairy cream cheese
1½ cups cheddar cheese OR Daiya shreds
2 tablespoons nutritional yeast (optional)
1 teaspoon garlic powder
½ teaspoon turmeric
½ teaspoon pepper
1 teaspoon sea salt
½ cup cheddar cheese or Daiya (optional)

Servings 8, Calories 327, Carbohydrates 30.6g, Protein 12.2g, Cholesterol 33mg, Sodium 621mg, Fiber 4.2g, Sugars 5.5g

This is a great main dish casserole that is easy to make ahead. If you would like to make it even heartier, try adding in 8 ounces of cooked tempeh or sausage.

Zucchini & Quinoa Casserole

Instructions:

1. Preheat oven to 350 degrees.

2. Spray a medium skillet with olive oil and heat to medium. Add chopped onion and cook for five minutes. Add peppers and zucchini and cook for 8 more minutes. Stir in green chilies, corn, and cooked quinoa.

3. Meanwhile, melt butter in a saucepan and whisk in flour. Cook for 3 minutes, until brown. Whisk in milk. Cook over medium heat until thickened, about 4 or 5 minutes. Add cheese, cream cheese, nutritional yeast, smoked paprika, and salt and cook until cheese is melted.

4. Combine quinoa mixture with cheese sauce and top with additional cheese. Bake for 15 minutes and allow to cool for 10 minutes prior to serving.

Olive oil spray
1 yellow onion, chopped
½ green pepper, chopped
½ red pepper, chopped
3 zucchini, shredded
4 ounces chopped green chilies
1 cup frozen corn, thawed
3 cups cooked quinoa
3 tablespoons quinoa flour
2 tablespoons butter or olive oil
1 cup unsweetened almond milk (or milk of choice)
8 ounces Havarti cheese or Daiya Havarti, shredded
4 ounces dairy or nondairy cream cheese
¼ cup nutritional yeast (optional)
½ teaspoon sea salt
½ teaspoon smoked paprika
½ cup mozzarella cheese or Daiya mozzarella

Calories 385, Fat 19.3g, Carbohydrates 46.8g, Protein 11.3g, Cholesterol 0, Sodium 624mg, Fiber 11.3g, Sugars 9.3

This is a great make-ahead dish!

Broccoli & Quinoa Stuffed Potatoes

Instructions:

1. Preheat oven to 400 degrees.

2. Place scrubbed potatoes directly on the rack and bake for about 1 hour, or until soft.

3. Meanwhile, in a medium bowl combine quinoa, sour cream, chopped broccoli, cheese, Italian seasoning, salt, and pepper.

4. When potatoes are done, allow to cool slightly. Lower oven to 375 degrees. Line a rimmed baking sheet with parchment paper.

5. Slice potatoes in half and scoop out, leaving ¼-inch shell. Mash potatoes with a fork and add to the quinoa broccoli mixture. Stir until well combined.

6. Place the shells on the prepared baking sheet and fill with quinoa mixture. Top each potato half with a sprinkle of Parmesan cheese. Bake for 20 minutes.

7. Meanwhile, heat marinara over low heat until warm.

8. Top potatoes with marinara and serve warm.

4 medium baking potatoes, washed
1 cup cooked quinoa
½ cup low fat sour cream or vegan sour cream substitute
¾ cup broccoli, blanched and finely chopped
¼ cup shredded cheese or Daiya Shreds
½ teaspoon Italian seasoning
¾ teaspoon sea salt
½ teaspoon fresh ground pepper
¼ cup Parmesan or vegan Parmesan substitute
½ cup marinara

Servings 8, Calories 170, Fat 4.3g, Carbohydrates 28.5g, Protein 5.2g, Cholesterol 1 mg, Sodium 344mg, Fiber 4.1g, Sugars 2.6g

Desserts

This is perfect topped with a scoop of vanilla ice cream!

Apple Pear Quinoa Crumble

Instructions:

1. Preheat oven to 400 degrees. Grease 8 six-to eight-ounce ramekins.

2. In a small bowl combine quinoa flour, quinoa, almonds, brown sugar, and cinnamon. Using a pastry cutter or the back of a fork mix in butter until coarse crumbs are formed.

3. In a large bowl combine pears and apples. Toss with sugar and flour. Add lemon juice and apple juice and stir until well combined. Place apple mixture in ramekins and top with streusel from step 2. Bake for 40 minutes.

½ cup toasted quinoa flour

½ cup cooked quinoa

¼ cup chopped walnuts
   or sliced almonds

¼ cup coconut palm sugar
   or brown sugar

¼ teaspoon ground cinnamon

3 tablespoons Earth Balance or
   butter, softened

3 medium apples, peeled
   and chopped

3 medium pears, peeled
   and chopped

2 tablespoons coconut palm
   sugar

1 tablespoon toasted quinoa
   flour

2 tablespoons lemon juice

¼ cup apple cider or apple
   juice

Servings 8, Calories 216, Fat 6.7g, Carbohydrates 29g, Protein 2.7g, Cholesterol 11mg, Sodium 41mg, Fiber 5.3g, Sugars 22.8g

This is truly a guilt-free dessert! I used all blueberries here, but a mixture of berries would be lovely.

Berries & Quinoa with Vanilla Bean Syrup

Instructions:

1. Using a sharp paring knife, split the vanilla bean lengthwise. Scrap out seeds with the back of the knife, reserving the empty pod for a garnish if desired. Put the seeds in a small saucepan along with sugar and ¼ cup of water. Bring to simmer over medium heat, stirring until sugar dissolves. Reduce heat to low and cook for 8 minutes. Strain through a fine strainer (the one you use to drain quinoa will work well). Let cool. Refrigerate until chilled.

2. Wash the berries and dry. If using strawberries, cut into quarters. Mix berries with quinoa and toss with just enough syrup to coat.

½ vanilla bean
¼ cup evaporated cane juice
   (or sugar of choice)
4 cups fresh berries
2 cups cooked quinoa

Servings 6, Calories 103, Fat 1.6g, Carbohydrates 20.1g, Protein 3.4g, Cholesterol 0mg, Sodium 2 mg, Fiber 5.9g, Sugars 3.3g

ookies are just as good as many conventional recipes, but a whole lot healthier!

Chocolate Chip Quinoa Cookies

Instructions:

1. Preheat oven to 350 degrees. Line a baking sheet with parchment paper.

2. Make flax eggs by combining two tablespoons organic flax seed meal (or ground flax seeds) with 6 tablespoons warm water. Set aside to thicken. (Skip this step if you are using eggs.)

3. In a large bowl combine almond meal, quinoa flakes, baking soda, and salt and stir until well combined. In a separate bowl, combine flax egg, almond butter, applesauce, maple syrup, and vanilla. Mix well and add to the quinoa and almond mixture slowly. Add in chocolate chips.

4. Using a tablespoon measure, drop cookies onto prepared parchment paper. Flatten slightly with clean fingers. Bake for 12 to 15 minutes, until lightly golden brown. Remove from oven and allow to sit in the pan for 5 minutes. Move to a cooling rack and allow to cool completely.

2 flax eggs (2 tablespoons flax seed meal combined with 6 tablespoons warm water) or 2 eggs

1 ¼ cups almond meal

1 cup quinoa flakes

¾ teaspoon baking soda

¾ teaspoon salt

½ cup almond butter (peanut or sunflower seed butter would work too)*

¼ cup applesauce

¼ cup maple syrup (or other liquid sweetener)

1 teaspoon vanilla extract

¾ cup chocolate chips

Servings 24, Calories 119, Fat 7.5g, Carbohydrates 10.7g, Protein 2.9g, Cholesterol 1mg, Sodium 118mg, Fiber 1.5g, Sugars 5.4g

If you do use sunflower butter, the cookies may turn green after cooling due to the chlorogenic acid. The solution is to reduce the baking soda in half. You can read more about it here: http://www.ochef.com.

azy as it may sound, these apple wedges are one of my favorite treats! I love the
olness of the apples combined with the crunchy coating.

Chocolate Quinoa Apple Wedges

Instructions:

1. Line a baking sheet with parchment or wax paper.

2. Combine lemon juice and water and add apple wedges. Toss to coat and set aside.

3. Heat coconut oil over medium heat. Add quinoa, oats, and coconut palm sugar. Toast stirring frequently for 5 to 7 minutes or until quinoa is golden brown. Place in a shallow dish and allow to cool slightly.

4. Place chocolate in the top of a double boiler over low heat. Stir until melted, making sure that no water reaches the chocolate.

5. Drain apple wedges on a paper towel. Carefully dip apple wedges, holding from the skin side. Alternately, you may use a spoon to spread the chocolate over the wedges, holding over the boiler to allow any excess to drip back. Place on the prepared baking sheet and sprinkle with quinoa mixture, pressing lightly so that it adheres. Refrigerate for 20 minutes, or until set. Store in the refrigerator.

1 tablespoon lemon juice

1 cup water

2 large apples, cut into wedges

1 tablespoon coconut oil

¼ cup quinoa, rinsed

¼ cup regular or gluten free oats

1 tablespoon coconut palm sugar

6 ounces chocolate, chopped fine

Servings 8, Calories 177, Fat 7.9g, Carbohydrates 28.5g, Protein 2.5g, Cholesterol 0mg, Sodium 5mg, Fiber 1.9g, Sugars 18.3g

e these with the chocolate drizzle, but my husband thinks they are better without. Give
em a try and decide for yourself.

Coconut Florentine Lace Cookies

Instructions:

1. Preheat oven to 350 degrees. Line 2 rimmed cookie sheets with foil. Grease foil and set aside.

2. In a medium saucepan, combine sugar, butter, coconut milk, and agave nectar. Cook over low heat for about 5 minutes or until sugar is dissolved, stirring near constantly.

3. Bring to a boil. To prevent sugar from crystallizing, brush down sides of saucepan with a wet pastry brush. Cook until thermometer registers 238 degrees. Remove from heat and immediately stir in quinoa flakes, quinoa, almonds, coconut, flour, lemon peel, and vanilla extract.

4. Drop by the tablespoon on prepared pans. (Keep about 3 inches apart.) With a fork dipped in cold water, flatten the cookies. Bake for 5 minutes. Switch racks and bake for 3 to 5 minutes longer.

5. Cool on baking sheets and then lift from foil. Place on a large sheet of parchment paper.

6. Place chocolate in the top of a double boiler and melt over simmering water. Stir in cayenne pepper. Drizzle cookies with chocolate and let sit until chocolate has set.

3/4 cup coconut palm sugar

1/2 cup Earth Balance or butter

1/3 cup canned coconut milk

2 tablespoons agave nectar or maple syrup

1/2 cup quinoa flakes

1/2 cup cooked quinoa

1 cup finely chopped almonds

1/2 cup shredded unsweetened coconut

3 tablespoons gluten-free all purpose quinoa flour blend

1/2 teaspoon grated lemon peel

1 teaspoon vanilla extract

Chocolate Drizzle (optional)

1/8 teaspoon cayenne pepper (optional)

4 ounces dark chocolate

Cookies: Servings 24, Calories 122, Fat 7.5g, Carbohydrates 12.8g, Protein 1.9g, Cholesterol 10mg, Sodium 42 mg, Fiber 1.1g, Sugars 6g

Drizzle: Servings 24, Calories 25, Fat 1.4g, Carbohydrates 2.8g, Protein .4g, Cholesterol 1mg, Sodium 4mg, Fiber 0g, Sugars 2.4g

These are a great healthy treat that kids of all ages love! The addition of sugar is completely optional—I find that the sweetness of the dates is enough for me. The boys, of course, say the sweeter the better.

Quinoa Date Snowball

Instructions:

1. Place coconut in a shallow dish. In a food processor combine dates, quinoa, almonds, sugar, cinnamon, vanilla, and sea salt. Process until smooth.

2. Form into very small balls, about ½ teaspoon in size. Roll the balls in the coconut pressing to coat as needed.

3 tablespoons unsweetened shredded coconut

5 ounces pitted dried dates

½ cup cooked quinoa

¼ cup raw almonds

1 tablespoon coconut palm sugar (optional)

½ teaspoon cinnamon

½ teaspoon vanilla

$1/8$ teaspoon sea salt

Servings 16, Calories 51, Fat 1.6g, Carbohydrates 9.3g, Protein .9g, Cholesterol 0mg, Sodium 18mg, Fiber 1.2g, Sugars 6.3g

Nothing says special occasion like a hot fudgy brownie! It is hard to believe that these are gluten-free and packed with quinoa.

Double Chocolate Quinoa Brownies

Instructions:

1. Preheat oven to 350 degrees.

2. Line a 9 x 9 square pan with parchment paper allowing the sides of the parchment paper to overlap the pan.

3. Place a metal bowl over a pot of simmering water and add dark chocolate and butter. Melt, stirring occasionally and being careful to not allow the water to touch the chocolate.

4. Meanwhile, place quinoa and flour in a blender. Process for 2 minutes. Add cocoa powder, salt, and baking soda. Process until smooth. Transfer to a large bowl.

5. If using flax eggs, combine 3 tablespoons ground flax seeds with ½ cup plus 1 tablespoon of warm water. Mix well and set aside to thicken.

6. In a medium bowl combine eggs (or flax eggs), coconut palm sugar, and maple syrup. Whisk until well combined. Add yogurt, coconut oil, vanilla extract, and melted chocolate.

7. Add wet ingredients to the quinoa mixture and stir until well combined. Stir in walnuts (optional). Place batter in prepared pan and bake for 30 to 35 minutes. Remove from oven and place pan on rack. Allow to cool completely. Use the parchment paper to lift brownies from pan. Cut and serve.

6 ounces dark chocolate, chopped
2 tablespoons Earth Balance or unsalted butter
1 ½ cups cooked quinoa
¾ cup gluten-free all purpose quinoa flour blend
¼ cup cocoa powder
¼ teaspoon salt
½ teaspoon baking soda
3 large eggs or flax eggs
¾ cup coconut palm sugar
¼ cup maple syrup
½ cup plain low fat or soy yogurt
¼ cup coconut oil, melted
2 teaspoons vanilla extract
¾ cup chopped walnuts (optional)

Servings 16, Calories 252, Fat 13g, Carbohydrates 30.4, Protein 5.1g, Cholesterol 41mg, Sodium 127mg, Fiber 1.6g, Sugars 15.9g

This is a favorite cookie around our house—and one I feel great about feeding the boys! To blanch whole almonds, boil water in a medium saucepan. Add almonds and cook for 1 minute. Drain and allow to cool slightly. Peel almonds. You may skip this step if desired.

Flourless Chocolate Quinoa Cookies

Instructions:

1. Preheat oven to 350 degrees. Line a baking sheet with parchment paper.

2. In a small bowl combine flax meal (or ground flax seeds), chia seed, and warm water. Whisk well and set aside. (Skip this step if you are using eggs.)

3. In a food processor combine almonds and quinoa. Process for 1 minute, or until you have a fine meal. Add baking soda and salt and process until blended.

4. Heat a small saucepan to medium low and add almond butter and coconut oil. Cook until coconut oil and almond butter are melted, whisking occasionally. Add in applesauce and maple syrup and whisk until heated through. Remove from heat and stir in vanilla and flax/chia eggs or eggs.

5. Add the warm almond butter mixture to your food processor and process until a dough has formed. Immediately add in the chocolate chips and process until chocolate is melted and blended, stopping to scrape down the sides as necessary.

2 flax/chia eggs (1 tablespoon flax meal + 1 tablespoon chia seeds + 6 tablespoons warm water) or 2 eggs
1 cup blanched almonds*
1 cup cooked quinoa
¾ teaspoon baking soda
¾ teaspoon salt
⅓ cup almond butter
1 tablespoon coconut oil
¼ cup applesauce
¼ cup maple syrup
1 teaspoon vanilla
¾ cup chocolate chips

6. Roll the dough into small balls and flatten with your fingers. (You could also use a fork.) Bake for 12 to 15 minutes. Allow to cool for 5 minutes in the pan and then transfer to a wire rack to cool completely.

Variations:

1. For double chocolate cookies, allow the batter to cool and stir in ½ cup vegan chocolate chips.

2. For chocolate macadamia nut cookies, stir in ½ cup chopped macadamia nuts just prior to cooking.

3. For cherry chocolate cookies, stir in ½ cup dried unsweetened cherries just prior to cooking.

Servings 12, Calories 163, Fat 11g, Carbohydrates 12.7, Protein 4.0g, Cholesterol 0mg, Sodium 231mg, Fiber 2.4g, Sugars 6.7g

I love this topped with a scoop of vanilla ice cream!

Blueberry Quinoa Crumble

Instructions:

1. Preheat oven to 350 degrees.

2. In a large bowl toss blueberries and quinoa flour. Place in a baking dish and dot with butter.

3. In a food processor combine quinoa flakes, cooked quinoa, pecans, salt, coconut palm sugar, evaporated cane juice sugar, melted coconut oil, and vanilla extract. Process until well combined.

4. Sprinkle topping over fruit and bake for 15 to 20 minutes. Serve with vanilla ice cream if desired.

4 cups fresh or frozen blueberries, thawed and rinsed

1 tablespoon toasted quinoa flour

1 tablespoon butter or Earth Balance

¼ cup quinoa flakes

¼ cup cooked quinoa

½ cup pecans

⅛ teaspoon salt

2 tablespoons coconut palm sugar (or brown sugar)

2 tablespoons evaporated cane juice sugar (or granulated sugar)

3 tablespoons coconut oil, melted

1 ½ teaspoons vanilla extract

Calories 258, Fat 15.9g, Carbohydrates 29g, Protein 2.6g, Sodium 78mg, Fiber 3.7g, Sugars 17.6g

My younger son loves these cookies—and I love that they are healthier than the store-bought alternative.

Quinoa-Flax Chocolate Chip Cookies

Instructions:

1. Preheat oven to 350. Line 2 baking sheets with parchment paper.

2. If using flax eggs, combine 2 tablespoons ground flax seeds with 6 tablespoons warm water. Mix well and set aside. (Skip this step if you are using eggs.)

3. In a medium bowl combine flour, quinoa flakes, flaxseed, baking soda, sea salt, and ground cinnamon.

4. Beat together the butter, applesauce, and sugars on medium high speed until fluffy, about 3 or 4 minutes. Add eggs, one at a time, ensuring the first is fully incorporated before adding the next. Add vanilla and reduce the speed to low. Add in flour and beat until just combined. Stir in chocolate chips.

5. Drop in teaspoonfuls onto prepared baking sheets. Bake for 9 to 11 minutes. Let the cookies cook for 4 minutes on the baking sheets and then transfer to racks to cool completely.

1 ½ cups gluten-free all purpose quinoa flour blend (see p. 30)

1 cup quinoa flakes

¼ cup ground flaxseed

1 teaspoon baking soda

1 teaspoon sea salt

½ teaspoon ground cinnamon

1 stick unsalted butter or coconut oil, softened

½ cup applesauce

1 cup coconut palm sugar (or sugar of choice)

½ cup packed dark brown sugar

2 large eggs or flax eggs

1 ½ teaspoons vanilla extract

1 cup semisweet chocolate chips

{ 1 cookie, Calories 150, Fat 6.2g, Carbohydrates 21.7g, Protein 2.1g, Cholesterol 21mg, Sodium 145mg, Fiber 1.5g, Sugars 13.1g }

is a gluten-free treat that my boys love!

Chocolate Mint Ice Cream Sandwiches

Instructions:

1. Place chocolate and coconut oil in the top of a double boiler. (A metal bowl on top of a sauce pan works too.) Melt over medium low until smooth. Remove from heat and allow to cool.

2. Meanwhile, sift together flour, cocoa powder, baking soda, and salt.

3. In the bowl of an electric mixer, combine the sugar, applesauce, (flax) eggs, mint extract, and vanilla. Beat for 2 ½ minutes on medium speed. Reduce speed to low and add the chocolate. Add flour mixture until just combined. Transfer mixture to a bowl and refrigerate for (at least) 1 hour.

4. Line 2 baking sheets with parchment paper. Preheat oven to 325 degrees. Form 16 balls with the cookie dough. Divide the balls between the 2 cookie sheets and flatten slightly. Bake for 15 minutes, rotating the trays half way through. Let cool for 5 minutes on the pan and then transfer to a wire rack to cool completely.

5. Allow the ice cream to soften and then spread onto the flat side of one of the cookies. Top with another cookie and wrap with parchment paper, wax paper, or plastic wrap. Freeze for 1 hour, or until firm.

1 cup semisweet chocolate chips

⅓ cup coconut oil

1 cup gluten-free all purpose quinoa flour blend (see p. 30)

3 tablespoons unsweetened cocoa powder

¾ teaspoon baking powder

¼ teaspoon sea salt

½ cup coconut palm sugar

¼ cup applesauce

2 eggs or flax eggs, at room temperature

1 teaspoon vanilla extract

½ teaspoon mint extract

Mint chocolate chip or vanilla ice cream

Servings 8, Calories 344, Fat 18.6g, Carbohydrates 43.8g, Protein 3.4g, Cholesterol 41mg, Sodium 102mg, Fiber 2.6g, Sugars 25.6g
Not including ice cream.

Ahh! Nothing says fall like the smell of baked apples in the oven. Although these are special enough for dessert, I've been known to enjoy them for breakfast.

Quinoa Baked Apples

Instructions:

1. Preheat oven to 325 degrees

2. Using an apple corer or paring knife, remove cores of apples to ½ inch of the bottoms of the apples. Make the holes wide enough for stuffing.

3. In a small bowl mix quinoa, rolled oats, walnuts, palm sugar, quinoa flour, and cinnamon.

4. Stuff cored apples with quinoa mixture. Place in a casserole dish and dot with Earth Balance or butter. Pour apple juice in the bottom of the dish. Bake for 45 minutes to 1 hour. Allow to cool slightly before serving and top with ice cream or yogurt if desired.

6 baking apples (Like Golden Delicious or Granny Smith)
¼ cup cooked quinoa
2 tablespoons rolled oats
¼ cup chopped walnuts
¼ cup coconut palm sugar
1 tablespoon toasted quinoa flour
½ teaspoon cinnamon
2 tablespoons Earth Balance or butter
1 cup apple juice

{ Servings 6, Calories 229, Fat 7.6g, Carbohydrates 41.8g, Protein 2.4g, Cholesterol 10mg, Sodium 49mg, Fiber 5.2g, Sugars 29.5g }

I recommend storing these in the refrigerator. If your family likes these as much as mine does, you may find yourself storing them in the back of the refrigerator so they will last longer.

Salted Quinoa Chocolate Bark with Pistachios

Instructions:

1. Line an 8-inch pan with parchment paper. Mix melted chocolate with cayenne pepper and stir well. Pour chocolate in to prepared pan and smooth with a dry spatula. Top with popped or toasted quinoa, pistachios, and sea salt.

2. Chill for 30 minutes, or until set. Remove from pan and break into pieces.

8 ounces good quality chocolate, melted (I used Green & Black's dark chocolate)

$1/8$ teaspoon cayenne pepper, optional

$1/4$ cup popped quinoa (see p. 31)

$1/2$ cup shelled pistachios, chopped

$1/4$–$1/2$ teaspoon sea salt

{ Servings 6, Calories 152, Fat 9.8g, Carbohydrates 12.8g, Protein 4g, Cholesterol 0mg, Sodium 139mg, Fiber 3g, Sugars 6g }

This cake is best served warm!

Streusel Quinoa Cake

Instructions:

1. Preheat oven to 325 degrees. Grease pan well with coconut oil or butter. If using flax eggs, combine ground flax seeds with warm water and set aside for a gel to form.

2. Place cooked quinoa and flour in a food processor. Blend for 2 minutes, until well combined. Add brown sugar, cinnamon, and salt. Blend until well combined. Transfer to a bowl. Add nuts, quinoa, and butter and mix with a fork or your hands until the crumble comes together.

3. Sift together flour, baking powder, baking soda, cinnamon, ginger, and sea salt. In a large bowl beat together butter, applesauce, and coconut palm sugar until thick. Add (flax) eggs one at a time, blending as you go. Add yogurt, milk, and vanilla and blend until well combined.

4. Stir in sifted flour and blend until just combined.

5. Spoon half of batter into prepared pan. Top with 1 cup of streusel topping. Spoon remaining batter over and smooth the top. Top with remaining streusel.

6. Bake for about 1 hour and 10 minutes, or until a tester comes out clean. Place the pan on a wire rack and allow to cool for 10 minutes. Run a knife around the edges of the pan and remove the sides.

{ Servings 24, Calories 250, Fat 8g, Carbohydrates 39g, Protein 5.2g, Cholesterol 27mg, Sodium 254mg, Fiber 1g, Sugars 14.8g }

Streusel Topping

½ cup cooked quinoa
¼ cup gluten-free all purpose or cake quinoa flour blend (see p. 30)
1 cup packed brown sugar or coconut palm sugar
1 tablespoon ground cinnamon
½ teaspoon salt
½ cup chopped nuts (walnuts, pecans, almonds)
¼ cup butter or Earth Balance, softened

Cake

2¾ cups gluten-free quinoa cake flour blend (see p. 30)
1 tablespoon baking powder
1 teaspoon baking soda
1 ½ teaspoons ground cinnamon
½ teaspoon ground ginger
1 teaspoon sea salt
½ cup butter, Earth Balance or melted coconut oil
1 cup applesauce
1¼ cups coconut palm sugar
3 eggs or flax eggs (3 tablespoons ground flax seeds + 9 tablespoons warm water)
1½ cups low fat or soy yogurt (plain or vanilla)
½ cup milk of choice
1 tablespoon vanilla extract

I love this treat at the holidays!

Quinoa Biscotti

Instructions:

1. Preheat oven to 350 degrees. Line a baking sheet with parchment paper. If using flax eggs, mix 3 tablespoons ground flax seeds with 9 tablespoons warm water. Set aside.

2. In a medium bowl sift together flour, baking powder, and salt. Stir in cooked quinoa.

3. In a large bowl, beat agave nectar and butter at medium until creamy. Add (flax) eggs slowly, scraping down the sides as needed. Add in vanilla, almond extract, and coconut oil.

4. Reduce mixer to low and add in flour mixture just until combined. Add in almonds and orange zest.

5. Use floured hands and shape dough into a loaf on parchment-lined baking sheet. Pat the loaves flat on top and smooth with the back of a spoon that had been dipped in cold water. Bake for 35 minutes and remove from oven. Allow to cool on the baking sheet. Reduce oven temperature to 325.

6. Use a serrated knife to cut loaves onto ½-inch slices lengthwise. Cut lengths to about 2 ½ to 3 inches long. Place the slices on the baking sheet and bake for 20 to 25 minutes, flipping after 10 minutes. Allow to cool on a wire rack for 1 hour prior to serving.

2 cups gluten-free all purpose quinoa flour blend (see p. 30)

1 teaspoon baking powder

¼ teaspoon salt

½ cup cooked quinoa

²/₃ cup agave nectar or maple syrup

4 tablespoons Earth Balance or unsalted butter, softened slightly

3 flax eggs or room temperature eggs

1 teaspoon vanilla extract

½ teaspoon almond extract

2 tablespoons melted coconut oil

2 teaspoons orange zest

¾ cup toasted almonds, chopped

Servings 24, Calories 132, Fat 4.8g, Carbohydrates 19.5g, Protein 2.5g, Cholesterol 5mg, Sodium 45mg, Fiber .6g, Sugars 5.4g

After one bite my husband declared that I'd captured the flavor of thin mints with these cookies (though obviously not the texture). I have to say I agree with him!

Chocolate Mint Cookies

Instructions:

1. Preheat oven to 350 degrees. Line a baking sheet with parchment paper.

2. Place 2 ounces of chocolate chips and cooked quinoa into a food processor. Process until smooth.

3. Sift together flour, cocoa powder, palm sugar, baking powder, baking soda and sea salt. Stir in quinoa mixture.

4. In a separate bowl combine coconut oil, maple syrup, applesauce, vanilla extract and mint extract. Whisk until well combined and add to dry ingredients. Stir until just mixed and add in remaining 2 ounces of chocolate chips.

5. Drop by the tablespoon to prepared baking sheet. Using a wet spoon, flatten the tops of the cookies. Bake for 12 to 18 minutes. Allow to cool for 5 minutes in the pan and then transfer to a rack to cool completely. If desired, top with mint drizzle.

6. To make mint drizzle combine all ingredients in a small bowl. Add additional milk by the teaspoon until desired texture is reached. Drizzle with a spoon onto cooled cookies. Alternatively, place icing in a small plastic bag and cut the corner to create an icing bag.

4 ounces chocolate chips, divided
½ cup cooked quinoa
1 cup gluten-free all purpose quinoa flour blend
¼ cup cocoa powder
¼ cup coconut palm sugar
1 teaspoon baking powder
½ teaspoon baking soda
¼ teaspoon sea salt
¼ cup coconut oil, melted
⅓ cup maple syrup
¼ cup applesauce
1 teaspoon vanilla extract
½ teaspoon mint extract

Mint drizzle, Optional

½ cup confectioners' sugar
½ tablespoon almond milk
½ teaspoon mint extract

Cookies: Servings 24, Calories 91, Fat 3.9g, Carbohydrates 13.3g, Protein 1.2g, Cholesterol 1mg, Sodium 56mg, Fiber .7g, Sugars 6.8g

Mint Drizzle: Servings 24, Calories 11, Fat .1g, Carbohydrates 2.5g, Protein 0g, Cholesterol 0mg, Sodium 0mg, Fiber 0g, Sugars 0g

Appendix: Salad Dressings

Finding gluten-free dressings that taste good and are healthy can be a challenge. Use these dressings to get creative and create your own quinoa salads.

Asian Dressing

Instructions:

1. Combine chia seeds and water in a small bowl. Set aside for 10 minutes. (Skip this step if you are using olive oil)

2. In a jar or blender, combine rice vinegar, lime juice, ginger, sweetener, soy sauce, miso, or salad and sesame oil (if using). Add chia seed mixture or oil and shake vigorously or blend. (If you are using miso I recommend using a blender to make sure it gets well combined.)

1 teaspoon chia seeds + 3 tablespoons water or 3 tablespoons olive oil

1 tablespoon seasoned rice vinegar

2 tablespoons lime juice

1 teaspoon minced fresh ginger

1 tablespoon agave nectar or coconut nectar

1 tablespoon soy sauce (or gluten-free tamari)

1 teaspoon mellow white miso (Optional: if not using, add in salt to taste)

2 teaspoons sesame oil (omit for oil-free version)

With Chia Gel: Servings 6, Calories 33, Fat 1.8g, Carbohydrates 4.2 g, Protein .4 g, Cholesterol 0 mg, Sodium 191 mg, Fiber .5, Sugar 2.7

With Oil: Servings 6, Calories 90, Fat 8.5g, Carbohydrates 4.2g, Protein .4g, Cholesterol 0mg, Sodium 197mg, Sugars 3.1g

Balsamic Vinegar Dressing

Instructions:

1. Combine water and chia seeds in a small bowl and set aside for 10 to 15 minutes, until a gel has formed. Skip this step if you are using oil.

2. Combine chia gel or oil and remaining ingredients in a blender or jar. Process until smooth. If desired, you may add in avocado, black olives, or flax seed oil for added thickness.

1 tablespoons chia seeds + ½ cup water or ½ cup olive oil

½ cup good quality balsamic vinegar

6 cloves of garlic, minced (more or less to taste)

1 tablespoon Dijon mustard

1 tablespoon maple syrup (optional)

¼ teaspoon crushed red pepper

½ teaspoon fresh ground black pepper

1 teaspoon sea salt

Optional: ½ avocado, ¼ cup black olives, ⅛ cup flax seed oil

{
Calories with chia gel only: Servings 8 (2 tablespoons), Calories 29, Fat .7g, Carbohydrates 5.3g, Protein .5g, Cholesterol 0mg, Sodium 250mg, Fiber .7g, Sugars 3.5g

Calories with ½ avocado: 49, Fat 2.5g, Carbohydrates 6.4g, Protein .8g, Cholesterol 0mg, Sodium 250mg, Fiber 1.6g, Sugars 3.6g

Calories with ¼ cup black olives: 34, Fat 1.1g, Carbohydrates 5.5g, Protein .6g, Cholesterol 0mg, Sodium 286mg, Fiber .9g, Sugars 3.5g

Calories with 1/8 cup flax seed oil: 41, Fat 1.4g, Carbohydrates 5.3g, Protein 1.2g, Cholesterol 0mg, Sodium 250mg, Fiber 1.7g, Sugars 3.5g

Calories with Oil: Calories 130, Fat 12.7g, Protein 2g, Cholesterol 0mg, Sodium 257mg, Sugars 3.5g
}

Chipotle Lime Dressing

Instructions:

1. In a small bowl combine water and chia seeds. Whisk well and set aside for 10 to 15 minutes until a gel forms. Skip this step if you are using oil.

2. Combine chia gel or oil in a jar or blender and add remaining ingredients. Shake or process until combined.

¼ cup water + 1 tablespoons chia seeds or ¼ cup olive oil

¼ cup lime juice

½–1 chipotle chile in adobo sauce (The dish will be HOT if you use 1)

4 cloves garlic, minced

½ cup fresh cilantro, chopped

1 teaspoon honey or agave nectar

1 teaspoon ground cumin

1 teaspoon sea salt

With Chia: Servings 4, Calories 37, Fat 1.7g, Carbohydrates 5.8g, Protein 1.4g, Cholesterol 1.4g, Sodium 552mg, Fiber 2g, Sugars 1.8g

With Oil: Servings 4, Calories 142, Fat 14.4g, Carbohydrates 4.8g, Protein .4g, Cholesterol 0mg, Sodium 531mg, Fiber .7g, Sugars 2.3g

Chipotle Thai Dressing

Instructions:

1. Combine water and chia seeds in a small bowl and mix well. Set aside and allow to sit for 10 to 15 minutes, until a gel forms. Skip this step if you are using olive oil.

2. Combine chia gel or oil and remaining ingredients in a jar or blender. Shake or blend until combined.

½ cup water + 1 tablespoon chia seeds or ½ cup olive oil

1 chipotle chili (from a can of chipotles in adobo)

3 cloves garlic, minced

3 tablespoons Thai sweet chili sauce

⅓ cup fresh lime juice

Servings 8 (2 tablespoons each)

With Chia Gel: Calories 26, Fat .8g, Carbohydrates 4.7g, Protein .6g, Cholesterol 1mg, Sodium 81mg, Fiber .9g, Sugars 2.4g

With Oil: Calories 125, Fat 12.8g, Carbohydrates 4g, Protein .2g, Cholesterol 1mg, Sodium 81mg, Sugars 2.4g

Cilantro Lime Dressing

Instructions:

1. In a small bowl combine water and chia seeds. Stir well and set aside for 10 minutes. (Skip this step if you are using olive oil.)

2. In a jar or blender, combine remaining ingredients and mix well. Add in chia gel or olive oil and shake or process until emulsified.

½ cup water + 1 tablespoon chia seeds or ½ cup olive oil

¼ cup fresh lime juice

2 tablespoons maple syrup (or other liquid sweetener)

2 tablespoons orange juice

1 jalapeño, seeded and diced

2 cloves garlic, minced

½ cup fresh cilantro leaves, chopped fine

1 teaspoon sea salt

{ With Chia: Servings: 8 (2 tablespoons each), Calories 27, Fat 7, Carbohydrates 5.5g, Protein .5g, Cholesterol 0mg, Sodium 235g, Fiber 18g, Sugars 3.5g

With Olive Oil: Servings 8 (2 tablespoons each), Calories 127, Fat 12.6g, Carbohydrates 4.8g, Protein .1g, Cholesterol 0mg, Sodium 235mg, Fiber 4.8g, Sugars 3.5g }

Honey Mustard Dressing

Instructions:

Combine all ingredients in a small bowl and whisk until well combined.

¼ cup honey or agave nectar

¼ cup Dijon mustard

1 tablespoon olive oil (optional)

2 tablespoons rice wine vinegar

½ teaspoon garlic powder or
   1 clove garlic, minced

½ teaspoon fresh ground
   black pepper

½ teaspoon sea salt

{ With Oil: Servings 8, Calories 56, Fat 2.1g, Carbohydrates 9.4g, Protein .4g, Cholesterol 0mg, Sodium 206mg, Sugars 8.8g

Omitting Oil: Servings 8, Calories 41, Fat .3g, Carbohydrates 9.4g, Protein .4g, Cholesterol 0mg, Sodium 206mg, Sugars 8.8g }

Orange Dijon Vinaigrette

Instructions:

1. In a small bowl combine water and chia seeds. Mix well and set aside for 10 to 15 minutes. Skip this step if you are using olive oil.

2. Combine chia gel or oil and remaining ingredients in a blender or food processor. Process until smooth.

½ cup water + 2 tablespoons chia seeds or ½ cup olive oil

¼ cup apple cider vinegar

¼ cup orange juice

2 tablespoons Dijon Mustard

1 tablespoon finely ground walnuts

1½ teaspoons orange zest

½ teaspoon sea salt

¼ teaspoon fresh ground black pepper

Servings 9 (2 tablespoons each)

With Chia Gel: Calories 30, Fat 1.8g, Carbohydrates 2.6g, Protein 1.1g, Cholesterol 0mg, Sodium 146mg, Fiber 1.3g, Sugars .7g

With Oil: Calories 109, Fat 11.9g, Carbohydrates 1.2g, Protein .4g, Cholesterol 0mg, Sodium 145mg, Sugars .7g

Southwestern Lime Dressing

Instructions:

1. In a small bowl combine water and chia seeds. Mix well and set aside for 10 to 15 minutes, until a gel forms. (Skip this step if you are using olive oil.)

2. In a jar or blender combine chia gel or oil and remaining ingredients. Process or shake until combined.

¼ cup water + ½ tablespoon chia seeds or ¼ cup olive oil

¼ cup lime juice

1 tablespoon agave nectar or honey

1 tablespoon hot sauce (more or less to taste/depending on hot sauce used)

1 teaspoon ground cumin

2 cloves garlic, minced

½ teaspoon sea salt

Servings 5 (2 tablespoons each)

With Chia Gel: Calories 27, Fat .6g, Carbohydrates 5.7g, Protein .5g, Cholesterol 0mg, Sodium 265mg, Fiber .6g, Sugars 3.7g

With Oil: Calories 106, Fat 10.2g, Carbohydrates 5.1g, Protein .2g, Cholesterol 0mg, Sodium 265mg, Sugars 3.7g

Sweet Spicy Dijon Dressing

Instructions:

1. In a small bowl combine chia seeds and water. Whisk well and set aside for 10 minutes or until a gel forms. (Skip this step if you are using olive oil.)

2. In a blender or food processor combine chia gel or olive oil and remaining ingredients. Process until smooth.

½ cup water + 1 tablespoon chia seeds or ½ cup olive oil

2 tablespoons apple cider vinegar

2 tablespoons Dijon mustard

½ chipotle chili in adobo sauce (use 1 for a VERY hot dressing)

2 tablespoons agave nectar, maple syrup or liquid sweetener of choice

3 cloves garlic, minced

½ teaspoon sea salt

½ teaspoon fresh cracked black pepper

Servings 5 (2 tablespoons each)

With Chia Gel: Calories 47, Fat 1.3g, Carbohydrates 8.7g, Protein 1g, Cholesterol 0mg, Sodium 259mg, Fiber 1.3g, Sugars 6.5g

With Oil: Calories 225, Fat 22.7g, Carbohydrates 7.5g, Protein .4g, Cholesterol 0mg, Sodium 259mg, Sugars 6.5g

Thai Dressing

Instructions:

In a small bowl combine chia seeds and water. Blend well and set aside for 10 to 15 minutes, until a gel forms. Skip this step if you are using olive oil. In a blender combine chia gel or oil and remaining ingredients. Process until smooth.

½ teaspoon chia seeds +
  2 tablespoons water or
  2 tablespoons olive oil
¼ cup seasoned rice vinegar
3 tablespoons lime juice
3 tablespoons tamari
  (use gluten-free if you are
  avoiding gluten)
1 tablespoon agave nectar
  (or sweetener of choice)
2 teaspoons toasted
  sesame oil
1 tablespoon sriracha hot
  chili sauce (make sure
  gluten free)
5 cloves garlic, minced (more
  or less to taste)
½ teaspoon pure Himalayan salt
¼ teaspoon fresh ground black
  pepper

{
Servings 7 (2 tablespoons each)

With Chia Gel: Calories 36, Fat 1.4g, Carbohydrates 5.2g, Protein 1.1g, Cholesterol 0mg, Sodium 651mg, Sugars 3.g,

With Oil: Calories 70, Fat 5.3g, Carbohydrates 5.5g, Protein 1g, Cholesterol 0mg, Sodium 660mg, Sugars 3.1g
}

A C K N O W L E D G M E N T S

First and foremost, a giant thank you to my husband Vincent. Thank you for the foot rubs, dried tears, and endless patience required of you as a result of me writing this book while pregnant. Thank you for always believing that I can do more than I think is possible. I love you and I like our city more and more every day.

Alex and Christian, thank you for being my reason. I am so proud of you both and savor every second we share. You are what makes my heart beat and fill me with joy, and I can only hope that one day you understand. Thank you for being my toughest food critics and for always pushing me to make healthy taste better.

To baby Skye, thank you for being with me every step of the way. I can't wait to meet you!

Dad, thank you for the countless kitchen clean ups. Mom, thank you for your attention to detail and being willing to overcome your dislike of quinoa and taste recipes for me. I'll make a quinoa lover out of you yet!

Lastly, to my readers and CookingQuinoa.net, thank you for making it all possible. It still surprises me that such an amazing group of people is actually reading my work. I love you guys!

Wendy

ABOUT THE AUTHOR

Wendy Polisi is the creator of CookingQuinoa.net, where she shares healthy creative recipes and celebrates all things quinoa. An avid cook from an early age, Wendy enjoys the challenge of creating dishes that are healthy without sacrificing flavor. She is the author of the bestselling *Quintessential Quinoa Cookbook* as well as popular ebooks *QuinoaFit and The Holiday Quinoa Cookbook*. Wendy's current projects include a follow-up to her first two books, *The Quintessential Dessert Quinoa Cookbook* and launching her first food blog not dedicated to quinoa, MamaBalance.com. Though she dedicates a great deal of time to all things food, her greatest accomplishment is being a homeschooling mom to two boys, ages 7 and 8. Presently she is looking forward to adding a little girl to the mix in the spring of 2013. Wendy is an avid promoter of lifestyle design and her family has been enjoying a location-independent lifestyle since 2008.

Connect:

Website: http://www.cookingquinoa.net

Facebook: https://www.facebook.com/CookingQuinoa

Twitter: https://twitter.com/cookingquinoa

Pinterest: http://pinterest.com/wendypolisi/

INDEX

METRIC AND IMPERIAL CONVERSIONS

(These conversions are rounded for convenience)

Ingredient	Cups/Tablespoons/Teaspoons	Ounces	Grams/Milliliters
Butter	1 cup=16 table-spoons= 2 sticks	8 ounces	230 grams
Cream cheese	1 tablespoon	0.5 ounce	14.5 grams
Cheese, shredded	1 cup	4 ounces	110 grams
Cornstarch	1 tablespoon	0.3 ounce	8 grams
Gluten-free flour, all-purpose	1 cup/1 tablespoon	4.5 ounces/0.3 ounce	125 grams/8 grams
Gluten-free flour, whole wheat	1 cup	4 ounces	120 grams
Fruit, dried	1 cup	4 ounces	120 grams
Fruits or veggies, chopped	1 cup	5 to 7 ounces	145 to 200 grams
Fruits or veggies, puroed	1 cup	8.5 ounces	245 grams
Honey, 100% pure maple syrup, or corn syrup	1 tablespoon	.75 ounce	20 grams
Liquids: cream, milk, water, or juice	1 cup	8 fluid ounces	240 milliliters
Oats	1 cup	5.5 ounces	150 grams
Salt	1 teaspoon	0.2 ounces	6 grams
Spices: cinnamon, cloves, ginger, or nutmeg (ground)	1 teaspoon	0.2 ounce	5 milliliters
Sugar, brown, firmly packed	1 cup	7 ounces	200 grams
Sugar, white	1 cup/1 tablespoon	7 ounces/0.5 ounce	200 grams/12.5 grams
Vanilla extract	1 teaspoon	0.2 ounce	4 grams

OVEN TEMPERATURES

Fahrenheit	Celcius	Gas Mark
225°	110°	¼
250°	120°	½
275°	140°	1
300°	150°	2
325°	160°	3
350°	180°	4
375°	190°	5
400°	200°	6
425°	220°	7
450°	230°	8